CW00569191

The Fearless Life Guide is an All To Love Project by M.J. Robertson

Books may be purchased in quantity and/or special sales by contacting All To Love at www. alltolove.com

Cover Photo by: Robin Beer. Cover Design by: Samuel Dowden and M. J. Robertson
Editing by: Frances Sullivan

The Fearless Life Guide
ISBN: 978-0-9957023-1-8

First Edition

Contents

Preface

This guide is written as an instructional manual for an online course. The 11 steps, 88 lessons, and 69 exercises have proven valuable to participants, and since a course is not for everybody, I wanted everybody to at least have access to the material.

The Fearless Life Tribe referred to in the guidebook are alumni of the course. They are explorers, travellers, and dreamers like you and me. Through them, I have witnessed the potential of this guide, and am humbled knowing that they have benefitted from it. Watching them claim their Fearless Life fills me with joy.

It is important for me to note that while writing the guide I consciously chose to avoid references to the learned scholars and voices of change I admire. It was because I wanted to stay true to my own voice. Here, I will tell you how grateful I am for the voices who speak out relentlessly for love, for enlightenment, and for conscious awareness. Without those who have the courage to shine, our world would be very dark indeed. I owe much to Louise Hay and Eckhart Tolle, Esther Hicks, Wayne Dyer and Deepak Chopra to name but five. There are many more, of course, and they continue to inspire me daily.

I continue to practice and work with the guide myself. It keeps me focussed and grounded. It also keeps me honest – I cannot ask you to do something I have not been able to do.

I hope you enjoy "The Fearless Life Guide" as much as I do.

You can learn more about the online course at www.alltolove.com. Once you have read "The Fearless Life Guide", please contact us at the All To Love website if you feel inspired to do so. We would like to get to know more about you.

Peace and love,

M. J.

About the Author - A Brief Background

I consciously surrendered my life to the Universe around the age of 19. I am not just saying that to sound holy. My surrender had nothing to do with holiness and everything to do with sheer desperation and utter (usually drunken) confusion. I could no longer bear the pain of the horror, violence, and apathy I saw in the world and knew my burning desire for peace was beyond myself alone. Fortunately, due to a sincere connection to my inner voice (and a mother who encouraged me to listen to it), I gave into the pain of unknowing, and cried silently to myself, "I give my life to you, Universe, All. That. Is. Tell me where to go and what to do. I will do it." From that point on, whenever I rationalised myself out of following my inner voice, or listened to other people, I suffered greatly for it.

Looking back, I know my suffering came from disconnection, from giving my inherent power to someone, or something, outside of me. Once disconnected, the wheel of insanity rolled round and round between pain, suffering, and delusion. I found myself diving into whatever brought pleasure and dulled me. My discontent continued to increase. Boredom became the norm. I know now that, on some level, I chose these experiences, because as I awaken, I realise that we all see a world that reflects back to us our inner conflict.

So, how did I reconnect? By becoming a self-responsible, sovereign being. How do you become self-responsible? By recognising you are the creator of everything you see and experience. I started by slowing down and paying attention. I started to take responsibility for everything in my day-to-day world. Everything.

Our current collectively agreed state of being is a distortion of Truth; therefore, it is a highly dysfunctional reality for many, including me. Over time however, with persistence, I began to feel my way home. People appeared to assist me, deeper insights revealed themselves, and I started to enjoy life again. I began to remember what it meant to be happy. Now, I find myself enjoying the ride immensely.

In my late teens and early twenties, I was having some crazy cool spiritual awakenings, profound insights, brilliantly vivid cosmic dreams and revelations. At the same time, I did not have a clue what was going on, who I was, or what I was meant to do with it all. Instead, I partied. Partying was an easy distraction that brought with it tantalising delusions of grandeur and complete escapism.

Growing up, "spiritual people" were marginalised and called names like weirdos, cuckoos, and dirty hippies and so on. I was scared of being one of them. I wanted to fit in with the cool kids and feel special. I wanted to be important, a star. But, I wanted to be heard, too.

The harder I tried to fit in, the more chaotic my life became. The more I followed the norm and denied my inner knowing, the more alienated I felt. I was lost, and yet, within me, there was a voice that spoke of love in a way that comforted me with the promise of a happy life. I only had to learn to trust it.

Over the last fifteen years, I have learned many lessons. I have learned how painful self-denial is, why slowing down is the key to transforming the world, and how profoundly important it is to recognise the insidiousness of the distorted, judgmental mind. Finally, I came to learn what alignment feels like. Its inner tranquillity, bliss, and flow is glorious. It is the incomparable feeling of connectedness, knowing we are all one, each a part of the other and together an integral part of all that is. Sounds too good to be true? Well, I am here to tell you, it is true and very, very good.

I have always had a deep desire to help, not just people, but the whole world! I want to help Mother Earth and all of her inhabitants. Heck, I want to help space and any E.T. types out there. My heart came into this world full of love and compassion, and the ability to sense what others feel. Despite depression, self-abuse, and times of resistance, I kept coming back to my search for more. I listened, asked, read, received and studied until finally feeling my way into my own beautiful paradise.

The purpose of this guide is to share how I cleared my mind and transformed my life into one I love and create deliberately. There is a great deal of inner work to be done to achieve this state of being but I believe the masses are ready to take the leap.

I welcome you to join me. Your loving new world is yours to unwrap like a gift to yourself for this lifetime. You just need to start, relax, and enjoy the ride.

Introduction

This guidebook is written with an intention to empower you to follow your dreams and carve your own path to paradise. Your ability to create a new reality lies in your desire to be free and live in peace. If you have a desire to live in peace, and to ultimately create a more balanced and harmonious world, then this guide will be of service to you.

All that you see outside of you is a projection of long held thoughts, and beliefs. Collectively, when we agree with things, they become, or at least appear, real. When reality changes, it is because the collective decides to view something from a different angle. We can all do that in our own lives. We have that same power to alter and redefine our reality by looking at things from a different angle. When we own that change, or embody it, we actually change our energetic vibration or frequency. That is when things get really cool. There will be more talk about this later on, of course, but I wanted to ensure you that you have it within you to change your life.

One intention I have is that the steps in the guide be clear and easy for as many people as possible. Another intention is that I remain guided by unconditional love in the creation of this guide.

Each step can stand alone as tools for healing, or merged together as a complete foundational guide to living in alignment. More than anything, I ask you to trust your own inner-knowing and use what feels good to you.

IMPORTANT: YOU ARE YOUR OWN MASTER. No one and no thing perceived outside of you has any power over you unless you choose to let it.

Absorbing the Material

There is no end to your depth. Within you are all the resources you will ever need. You alone hold the key to your own fearless life. Nothing is outside of you. Seems deep, right? Maybe even intense? It can be, especially in the beginning. This is why I need to highlight right away the importance of meditation. It is so useful to you right now. You must begin the slowing down process so that you can absorb this material with greater ease. In general, surely you are aware that meditation is having a huge impact on society. In truth, the practice of slowing down to meditate is helping global awareness accelerate. Along with meditation I recommend relaxation. Even taking a minute to walk mindfully through the grass can help you recalibrate so that you feel relaxed and centred. When relaxed we soften, and begin to heal and re-attune ourselves. This is where actions should come from, a centred, relaxed and loving place.

As for the overall guide and how to make it work best for you, my recommendation is this: Absorb each Step. Remember, there is no cheating because you will only ever be cheating yourself, and as you move along, some steps might feel easy while others may require further enquiry or study. Take it all at your own pace.

Over time, you may find yourself gravitating towards new people and letting go of others, not due to a lack of love, but rather of resonance. You simply do not resonate with certain folks anymore. This is natural when we decide to change. You may have already experienced this, but remember that there should be no judgment in this kind of change. Always choose to see others in their power, allow them to make their own choices, as you are making yours. We are not here to fix each other, we are only here to experience creation in our own unique way. I think it feels way better when we focus on loving each other unconditionally instead of trying to control or fix each other. So stay focussed on your own inner work and bless others in theirs.

Most importantly, commit to yourself deeply. On a core level, commit to your own joyful fulfilment and have faith you will find your way, because you will. Continue to practice what you have learned as you move through each Step and give yourself permission to explore what feels best to you. Make up your own empowering affirmations, find innovative ways of questioning your own thoughts, assumptions, and beliefs, and be willing to go further than you ever imagined possible.

Before we start the lessons, it is important for you to understand the foundation of the practice, so let us begin.

Daily Practice: The Foundational Pillars

Getting to Know Your Emotional Body

We all have one emotional body that encompasses the full spectrum of emotional energies or frequencies. Negative emotions are of a lower frequency while positive emotions are of a higher frequency. The experiences you desire to have on Earth, your preferences or purpose, will dictate what resonates with you and what does not. Note: The form of your preferences, as in, what they look like, does not matter, there is no judgment when it comes to energy. It is about how you feel when you are having an experience. Comparing yourself to other people will only limit your ability to expand, so avoid doing it.

Simply put, when you feel bad, anxious, angry, or jealous, for example, your emotional body is letting you know you are perceiving something in a way that is not in alignment with your best self. The better you feel, the more in alignment you are with your highest purpose. So, the more aligned you are, the higher your vibrational frequency is, and so on. It is called becoming aware, conscious, or even enlightened, but the word does not matter, it is just really cool. Furthermore, by doing this work, you are raising the collective frequency. Indeed, you are affecting the whole wide world. You are increasing the vibrational frequency within the global consciousness affecting positively an awakening which is bringing about massive changes in the world as we currently know it. If you resonate with this material, you are a part of this tribe. However, there are points to be mindful of regarding our emotions.

It is important to recognise the difference between denying your emotions, indulging them, engaging with them, and observing them from a detached, loving place while using your awareness to process them properly. The latter response is the one we desire to have and it means being committed to breathing through any emotional upheavals, detaching from thought, owning the emotion as your own, forgiving yourself, loving it all as the totality of your own experience, and then consciously transforming the heavy or dense emotion. In so doing, you continue to rise and break through the old barriers of separation into eventual freedom. This is a cyclical process, which we will discuss in Step 1, so do not let it daunt you. The process becomes easier over time and with regular practice.

As you have probably noticed, the world is a mess. By the world, I mean you, too. Not just you though, humans generally speaking are a mess...a vibrational mess. There is so much denial and guilt, misunderstanding and confusion that many are frozen, too muddled and fearful to move. They feel hopeless because they cannot figure a way out of the mess. Well, we are going to change that. By working with the emotional body, you will gradually transform the messy bits and find your essence, your shiny, star power. The challenge, especially early on, is what I like to call the emotional storms. Let me explain what these are. You will have a better chance of surviving if you are well prepared before the storms hit.

Allowing Emotional Triggers, Waves, and Storms

There are three categories of an emotional transformation process and they relate directly to the power and force with which they are experienced: triggers, waves and storms. Just like real storms, the intensity varies, but they do always pass and are usually followed by a peaceful calm and relief. They also leave behind clarity.

Before I go ahead with my explanation of emotional storms, there is something I want you to be aware of. I will not go into a great amount of detail but feel it is helpful to know that a lot of emotions come from what I refer to as "the karmic backlog". In other words, some emotional responses to things in the here-and-now come from another time, a distant past. It is helpful to know that you did not single-handedly create all the angst you are feeling. However, you still have to deal with it and when you change your responses and shift the backlog, you change the future.

So what do you do when you feel a negative emotional charge? You own it, detach from it, and begin to breathe through the emotion. It may be that through the space you are providing with your conscious awareness, more emotion begins to rise up within you. This is the wave and can be experienced as profound sadness, pain, rage, you name it.

Triggers will dissolve with relative ease, within minutes. They are usually quite delicate and subtle and can slip past you.

You will become more aware of triggers once you have processed some bigger waves and storms.

Waves may last a couple of hours, while storms, which you will learn to laugh at eventually, may last for days.

An emotional storm is a multi-layered, high intensity, emotional experience. It occurs when you observe an emotional reaction within your present moment conscious awareness, and then other emotions come up. If possible, it is best to be alone when the storm hits so you can more easily detach from any judgmental or attack thoughts, whether directed at yourself or another.

Once you can catch your thinking and are able to detach from your thoughts, which are likely blaming something or someone for how you feel, begin to focus on the breath as a way to consciously transform the emotions. Using the inhale, envision the breath is flooding light into the feelings. On the exhale, they are transformed. Some people call this clearing, releasing or letting go, although let's not get too fussy about the words, simply agree to the process as a way to raise your vibration.

Within the empty space of detachment and allowing your emotions to clear out during waves and storms, you may experience memories, visions, revelations, and insights. This is a promise of things to come as eventually higher level thoughts will be available. High level intuitive thoughts feel clear, loving, and peaceful. In the meantime, practice sitting with what is happening in your body, without judgments or labels, and allow the emotions to move through you. Expect to receive inner guidance and wisdom that will soothe the pain, and it will come.

This process is a healing practice and it is transformative. Our emotional body (which is us) is cleansing itself of toxic wounds and cellular imprints. These lower energies no longer serve the collective, so we must agree to transform or in some cases, dissolve them.

Post storm, you have undergone a subtle vibrational shift and with it comes clarity and a renewed strength (for having survived the emotional ordeal). You might also have a different perspective on a situation. For example, you may suddenly see your body in a better light, or feel differently towards certain people in your life. Whatever the case, whether the emotional storm is new to you or not, you will likely agree it is not particularly pleasant. However, it is worth the price paid for the miraculous results it brings. One good thing is the more you practice, the easier it gets.

For women, pay special attention to your cycle and attune more diligently around this time. As deeper wounds rise up to empower divine feminine energy, which the world needs so much more of, powerful threads of anger, shame, guilt and hatred will likely appear. Life is a paradox. We are collectively moving into greater love and light, but our darkness needs to be acknowledged. It is the yin/yang, night/day, good/bad nature of this reality. Accept it. You have as much darkness in you as light. What is different is that you are choosing to focus on your love and light frequencies now. By doing this, you shine more light into the darkness.

Make sure you are being brutally honest with yourself when addressing emotional triggers, waves or storms. You might experience fits of tension, you may need to scream, cry, or hear voices (yes, voices) that speak to you. Detach from it all and let it be. Make sure you stop blaming the external world for how you feel in all cases. Go within and own your own emotional wounds. This is the best you can do to change your world and the best chance humanity has to end the madness!

During an intense emotional storm ask for help from within. Pray, do whatever it takes to release the attack thoughts and disentangle from your external projection. Avoid talking about it until the emotional charge has dissolved completely. Talking about a problem only perpetuates the problem.

This is really important stuff when it comes to creating truly harmonious relationships. When we no longer blame other people for how we feel, and take responsibility, we let other people off the hook. That is HUGE. Some lovely people on the planet do it naturally. I had to learn it. I grew up in an environment where there were class divides, some people were considered better than others, and we were all expected to strive, achieve, conform, fit in. "You have to do whatever it takes to get by", "It is a dog eat dog world", or, "An eye for an eye" were the adages I heard. None of it ever made sense to me and it certainly did not make me feel good. Hence, my personal story of moving from a state of disempowered painful confusion into an empowered loving and abundant life was written.

The important thing is to refrain from indulging and wallowing in your emotions, and definitely do not identify with them. Allow them to be there, because they are - otherwise you are in denial - notice and then detach from your thoughts and circumstances while owning the emotions. Encourage yourself to forgive, love, and transform that emotional density into one that feels better by choosing a more loving perspective. The storm will pass eventually. However, if you freak out and get scared and decide to deny its presence, then you hold onto it and delay the storm for another day.

This stuff makes sense to me and I believe it will make sense to you. I believe this is a collectively agreed upon process to help clean up the vibrational mess we are in. As we do the work, we permission others to do it, too, and help many more take that quantum leap into a loving new world.

Health: Mind/Body/Spirit Your Oneness Connection

In the world of judgment, our body is a separate, feared thing, which gets sick and dies. We are taught that the body must be managed by physical strength, discipline, and willpower. The mind is an ever evolving phenomenon and the spirit is pretty much denied altogether, especially in modern western civilisation. This is why there is so much conflict in the world, because we are fearful of the body, confused about the mind's potential, and in denial of the importance of a deeper spiritual connection.

In unity, there is no separation. Spirit is mind, mind is body. Together, you have this emotional body, which is energy in motion. Everything is energy and so the emotional body is you, and the sum total of your experiences here. To get to know yourself better, you must begin to honour and feel and listen to this subtle body. The mind is like the interface between spirit and form, it allows us to have this perceptual 'separate' looking experience, which is so cool. However, if the mind is being manipulated then your reality becomes distorted and a distorted mind distorts the body and the world you perceive.

Our own evolution is waking up to the truth of our "oneness". The Internet is an easy and rich resource for scholarly papers linking illness to emotions and thoughts. Simply put, if you deny these links, you stay sick. If you take responsibility, you heal. I encourage you to own your life completely while fine tuning to your intuition when it comes to your body's well-being. Always see a medical professional if you are being guided to. Medicines are a blessing and are not to be demonised, however, we need to use them with much more awareness instead of feeding them to a population in denial (or wildly mislead) in order to make a profit.

Look within yourself and own every bit of your experience. Start to engage in a dialogue with your body and use your awesome mind to expand how you feel and think about your body's functions and how it moves through time and space.

Well-being is, first and foremost, being in love with yourself and life. When in a place of well-being; joyful movements, healthy eating, contribution to others, and harmonious relationships flow.

Be kind to yourself throughout this and all processes you undertake and have no doubt that as you harmonise your inner world, your body will become a radiant example of that expanded awareness.

By choosing to embark on this journey, you are consciously empowering and enlightening not only your vibrations, but those of the entire human race. As you transform your low frequency energy to a higher energy, a ripple is created. Your energy is always sending out a vibration. As you move with the energy of hope, peace, and love, that energy is strengthening all those similar vibes in the collective. You are helping to shine light on control, domination, and greed, energies which do not serve humanity. It sounds simple and it is, although first you have to start noticing areas of your day to day life that might be holding you down. It is time to unplug.

Unplug

0.1 What to Unplug From

I am aware that many of you reading this are unplugged already, which is great. If, however, you are not, know that unplugging will greatly increase your ability to live peacefully. Let me explain.

Much of what we consume via mainstream media is filled with derisive, not to mention, violent and demoralising content. Advertisements are psychologically crafted tools designed to manipulate the masses' psyche. Of course, that is not true of every single program, and not all advertisements are going to turn you into a purchasing zombie. However, unplugging can help you figure out the overall affect the deluge of information coming at you is having. I would ask that even the news, which some argue has devolved into nothing more than sensational infotainment, be taken off your radar, at least while reading this book.

So yes indeed, I am telling you to turn off the news and stop watching television – all of it – which includes radio news, newspapers, and gossip magazines. To be clear, I am referring to all TV shows with advertising, and all mainstream news sources, soaps, reality shows, shock docs, and even some movies may be worth cutting out, like the senselessly violent ones or those which perpetuate limiting social conventions, for example.

I love movies, so do not get stuck on rules about what you can and can't watch when it comes to film, but do be aware of how stuff makes you feel. Even romantic comedies can create a sense of longing, which does not really serve your vibes and violent films can create a great deal of stress in the body, which isn't great either. Tip: If you are not enjoying a film, turn it off or leave the room.

Social media. Once you are unplugged from the mainstream, be diligent with how much time you spend on social media and turn it off if you notice yourself getting depressed or enraged. You are responsible for how you feel, so do not get sucked into social media if it bums you out. If you want to, come off it completely, your life will go on without it. You can always go back when you feel better able to gauge your responses with respect to it.

Please know, unplugging is not about demonising the world of entertainment, or TV, but rather it is about recognising our part in engaging with that which dumbs us down. Now, more than ever, it is important that we begin to redefine who we are, what we are doing here, and how we relate to one another and this planet. We begin by inner exploration, quieting the mind, and withdrawing from the external, which includes the teley-o!

We are all powerful and sacred creators. Much of what we see and hear from media hardens us, instils fear, and the result is apathy. Unplugging allows for a recalibration, giving you the opportunity to look at yourself through your own eyes. So plan to swap that TV time for the all-important-and-super-awesome 'going inward' time.

Going inward does not just mean sitting in meditation all day. It is mainly about authentic, creative self-exploration and the resulting expression. As we head into a brand new now, many will be feeling a pull to rediscover gifts and unique creative abilities. All of us have a purpose and we cannot truly embody it until we know inwardly who we are and what we are meant to be doing. Straight up, if you feel stuck, angry, bitter, or any combination of those feelings, your emotional body is telling you, you are out of alignment with your life's purpose. Until you change your focus, and permission yourself to enjoy life and fulfil your purpose, those feelings of stuck, angry, bitter and so on will remain habitually in place and more than likely get worse. But here is some good news.

At this time there is a critical mass of human beings moving with conscious awareness into higher frequency states. This is a beautiful thing and we are all a part of it. Former paradigms of fear, enslavement, limitation and oppression are being transformed with love, establishing in place of the old, a world of compassion, understanding, and unity. We are living at a time of massive evolutionary quantum leaps. It is the greatest story we have ever told and a miraculous thing to behold.

Our bodies are perfect conduits for love and light and we must use this awareness now. If unplugging seems an unrealistic option for you, at least begin to cut down, turn the volume down, stop watching commercials, read or meditate, and be more aware of how what you are watching makes you feel. If you notice something is making you feel bad, stop engaging with it. Be choosy with what you consume. Doing this will penetrate other areas of your life that involve consumption and help you make wiser choices that will benefit you and others.

Most importantly, recognise you have a choice in every moment. If at any point along the way you feel the TV, radio, magazine or newspaper is making you feel sad, lonely, scared or depressed, UNPLUG it.

0.2 Withdrawal

You are hooked on media drama, and depending on your degree of consumption, you will crave its fix. Just like any physical addiction, it is important for you to recognise that the media is affecting you, energetically and subliminally. Unplugging is one of the most powerful things you can do to expand, and decompress.

Over the next few months, you are going to be busy absorbing this material and doing inner work, so reach out to The Fearless Life Tribe if you start feeling anxious around this whole unplugging thing. Find like minds to support you and encourage your transformation.

If you really can't imagine not engaging with the mainstream media, perhaps this book is not right for you at this time. That is okay, you are always welcome to come back when you feel ready and able to unplug.

0.3 What To Expect

When you unplug, the world begins to look different. You gradually become more aware of your own thoughts and your own ideas about life, which may differ from what you have been hearing, or even what you believed those thoughts and ideas to be. Your mind will become clearer and soon you will feel the tasty delights of freedom. Your need to consume will be replaced with a desire to create.

Once unplugged, you might find you gravitate to different foods, fashion, or lifestyle choices. A lot of the TV being broadcast is super heavy, which makes it harder for us to lighten up and notice all the wonder and awesomeness of life because we have gotten trapped in a constructed illusion of what we should want, and worse, who we should be. Once unplugged for a while, you will notice your mind is less noisy, and on top of that, many of your less than desirable behavioural patterns will fall away. New, inspired thought will appear in your mind and you will have plenty of extra time.

If you are committed to becoming your best self, and know what it will mean to you and all of humanity, unplugging will not be so bad. The rewards are beyond what you can probably imagine at this point.

Take as much time as you need, when you are ready to unplug you can get started with the really wonderful work ahead. What are you waiting for?

Foundational Pillars

Exercise A.

Write down the range of emotions you feel on a regular basis.

Now, write down how you desire feeling on a regular basis. While doing this exercise, notice if any images come up. For example, do you see yourself gardening, dancing or spending time with loved ones?

Unplug

Exercise A.

Choose a program you watch regularly (weekly, daily, etc.) Ideally, something that your friends and family watch as well.

On your chosen day, refrain from watching it, sit with the TV off, don't do anything else instead and sit still doing nothing and see how long it is before you 'have' to begin to watch it. Or perhaps it was easy.

Exercise B.

Put your phone face down in front of you and note the time. Start to read a book or some other non-digital thing, and note the amount of time passed when you 'have' to check it.

Exercise C.

If you play phone or video games every day. Go one day without playing any games and notice how many times you think about it.

Exercise D.

On a weekday, avoid listening, watching or reading any news until midday, if possible, stop engaging completely for 3 days and notice the following things:

1) Was it more difficult to engage in conversation with co-workers?

2) Did you feel "out of the loop"?

4) Did you feel any different?

The following eleven steps outline an inner process for transformation. A shifting inner dialogue gradually alters lower energy vibrations and enhances the higher ones. By diligently practicing and eventually embodying many of the qualities discussed, your most miraculous life will unfold. You are on a journey to your dream life.

Step 1. Joy, Gratitude & Love

1.1 The System

Practicing gratitude is a great way to harness more love and joy. It is the direction we need to move in for greater harmony on the planet. Let's begin practicing right from the start. This lesson is going to show you how to start generating higher vibrations by becoming more inspired and loving. One way to get there is by unplugging, as already discussed. Another is by becoming aware of "the system" and your various responses to it.

I do not want to spend oodles of time on this subject so consider this an introductory primer of sorts. Suffice it to say we have all played a part in creating the system. Call it "the man", "the machine", or "old paradigm" it matters not. The system is that faceless, over-bearing, and oppressive establishment which we believe we "…cannot fight…" Mass media is a part of it now, too. Here's the thing. Let's stop fighting it. What?

Here is what I suggest. Right now, as you are reading this, start being grateful instead of angry or frustrated. Express gratitude for those institutions you feel have a stranglehold on you. Release that image and replace it with one of you holding it in a loving embrace. You have the power in you to be grateful for every single thing in your life and will be surprised how that seemingly simple act can dismantle the most monolithic of obstacles.

Once you are no longer fearful of the system, and can catch yourself when blaming "it" for this or that, you will begin to recognise your part in its creation, your support of it, and your place in its function. When you take responsibility and come from a place of gratitude, you begin to create something different. Visualising an altered system, one made up of higher vibrations, is easier when looking at it all through a lens of gratitude. And guess what? You are actually doing it now by unplugging and practicing being grateful. But what about joy and love?

Joy and love are the incredible perks of gratitude. You cannot have a heart filled with gratitude and not feel love and joy, too. It is simply not possible.

1.2 Vibrational States

"If you wish to understand the Universe, think of energy, frequency and vibration." Nikola Tesla

You are made up of trillions of vibrating active light particles which are infinitely connected to the entire Universe. Everything you feel, think, say and do is made up of a certain vibration or combination of energetic frequencies. If you are like me, you grew up in a world where you were taught, "This is how life is. This is how life works. You are going to follow these rules, get to this point at which time you will do that, then this, then that, until *poof* you are done. Your life is over." I could not buy into those projections. Whenever I tried, my life spiralled into despair. I'll bet many of you are the same. You grew up feeling squashed and alienated by these teachings.

Because energy is always in motion and can never be static, and your being is a vast spectrum of vibrational states, from super low to super high, you need to stay aware enough to distinguish the ones you desire versus the ones you want to re-move or transform. That just makes good sense. It follows then that what you see in your external world is an indicator of the vi-brations you are dominantly carrying. That is correct. If your world is chaos, you are vibrating chaos. If your world is full of serendipitous events, you are vibrating a positive openness to events around you.

Reflect briefly on the people, places, and things in your life that make you happy. Feel your heart expand with joy, grati-tude, and love. Now, think about some troublesome areas of your life. Friends or family members that drain you. Anxiety you feel around money perhaps. Stress you feel about your body, reputation, or job. Do you feel a restriction in your heart area? You have squeezed out all that joy and it does not feel good at all. So, pay attention to those two spectrums. Give yourself credit for all the areas of your life that feel good and know without doubt that the areas you do not feel good about are the challenges you are going to rise above.

The responses you have in any given situation are all connected to the emotional body which acts as a guidance system. As you learn and develop new skills in how to better relate to your emotions, raising yourself up will get easier and easier. You will cope with the emotional storms with greater love and compassion, and this too, will begin to exponentially expand your vibrational awareness making it easier to stay in a state of gratitude.

It is really important not to judge the vibration you are in, ever. Being quietly aware is more than enough to make the necessary changes. Judging will only block your potential, so do not judge. This judgment thing is a huge barrier for humanity's expansion and it needs further discussion, so I will go into greater depth about it in the next Step. On that note, somewhat paradoxically, it is important to stop thinking you know what is best for other people, let alone the world, right now. Stay focussed on your own vibes. That is all and it is plenty. Once you have sorted out your own vibrational mess, you will be clearer and making decisions and choices will be easier. Until then, have faith that all is as it should be. Take the pressure off yourself.

Putting pressure on yourself does not help. Just feel into that word, pressure. It is tension building. Tension is not useful when it comes to increasing your vibrations. Go the other way instead, practice being really easy about all this. Good vibes are heightened when you are relaxed. The well-being community and conventional medical community tell us to relax more. There are countless sources telling us that when relaxed we are more efficient, able to heal, and so on. Still it seems a hard thing for people to do. There are too many mixed messages. Relaxation is too often turned into escapism, which we can observe in modern party scenes and mind-numbing mainstream media consumption.

Hard partying and watching TV is not relaxation, but rather denial of, and escape from, a perceived reality. Simply put, people do not want to own up to how they really feel because it requires them to feel it, and make a change. Many continue to numb themselves over and over again and pretend everything is okay. They hide their suffering beneath sparkly party dresses or zone out in front of a TV screen.

Celebrate your life authentically. You can party and have loads of fun without getting totally obliterated. Find something to watch that is life affirming, uplifting. Monitor your own vibration as you engage with different environments and remind yourself that everything is vibrating. Of course, there is no judgment against the party people, celebration is sacred. However, escapism is something different. Become aware of any patterns of escapism and be willing to lift the lid on the emotions that lay underneath.

1.3 Patterns

We are surrounded by patterns of one form or another. There are patterns in nature, in great architectural designs like the pyramids, in cellular activity. The Earth orbits the Sun in a cyclical pattern. Vibrations form waves. Those waves form a frequency which is important because it allows energy to become form - any form. More specifically, every biological or non-biological thing has a unique energy signature that vibrates at certain frequencies. You have your own signature frequency as does "the system" and everything else. Reading this book is giving you the opportunity to expand beyond the system's pattern and align instead with your signature pattern so you can live fearlessly in love and abundance.

Really? How so? Let me explain.

I assume you all brush your teeth in the morning alongside specific morning rituals like taking a shower, eating breakfast, and getting dressed. Many of your patterns, like showering, are great, right? Keeping clean is useful and it feels good. Except when you are ten years old and all you want to do is play. I can remember my parents, one hot summer day, looking at me funny, telling me I needed to take a bath. I was a stinky kid because playtime was the only priority. I digress, but I learned then that showering is an important pattern to establish if you do not want people to pinch their noses around you.

I am sure you will agree, that while there are good things you do every day, there are a few things you do routinely that are not so good for you. And you know it because you feel bad about it. It is those 'bad' feelings and the thoughts aligned with those 'bad' vibes that you need to start paying attention to, not the behaviour itself.

Know this: Your behavioural patterns will shift when you transform whatever energy created the behavioural impulse in the first place. In order to do that you have to pay very close attention to your emotional reactive patterns and the thoughts that come up with the emotion. In order to make any changes in your life you must first become aware of what you want to change. Instead of beating yourself up for stuff you do that you think is bad, honour your desire to make change and choose to be kind to yourself always.

From this day forward, you are going to pay attention to your feelings, owning and honouring them. Take note, literally write it down, when co-workers, family, friends or circumstances trigger an emotional response. Whenever you start to feel stressed, sad, or experience any other low frequency emotion, write it down. The most important thing is that you do not react. When we react rather than respond, we deflect the potential for transformation and negative patterns remain locked in place. As mentioned, these patterns will only get worse. When, however, we allow even the ickiest of feelings to be noticed in any given moment, we weaken them giving way for our transformation and their dissolution.

Please remember, there is no good or bad when it comes to emotions. There is just you and how you feel and think about what you are experiencing. If it does not feel good to you, your emotional body is indicating your perception of a situation is not in alignment. Therefore, you do not resonate with it.

Once you begin to recognise your patterns, you can begin to pre-empt, or prepare for them. This will make your non-reactivity easier. Over time, as you take responsibility for all of your emotions, you will naturally begin to reframe your thinking. An important point to note here is you cannot live a fearless life unless you are aware of exactly what is stopping you from that life.

When we pay close attention to our emotional state and let ourselves feel into feelings, over time it becomes obvious that railing against our external reality is reactive and in all likelihood actually strengthening heavier or lower frequency patterns. When you pay attention to emotional triggers, you begin to own them and become responsible for them. Once you accept responsibility for all your feelings, you can begin to dissolve the negative emotional patterns as and when they arise.

You know now that you need to feel your emotions in order to transform. Keep reminding yourself to big yourself up for all the good feelings, and keep practicing gratitude as much as you can.

If stress patterns are showing up at, or around work, or with a partner, or a friend, take notice, it might be that you need a little distance for a while. Or maybe you notice you get anxious and feel bad about yourself whenever you go to the gym. I am not saying to stop exercising, but be willing to explore different ways of moving your body and simply notice the different feelings that arise when you try new things.

Many of our most powerful reactive patterns pivot around body image, the opposite sex, and money. Try this: When you get an electricity bill, notice how you feel. Breathe and allow whatever is going on inside you to go on. Are you worried? It is okay but now, be grateful! Tell yourself how thankful you are for your warm home, your hot water, and all those wonderful electric conveniences. Sit with the emotional charge, and keep breathing deeply while applying gratitude in the place of worry, until the worry is gone. Then, pay that bill with a big dollop of love. Do this every time, with every worry, and before you know it, you will have shifted your frequency around paying bills, and opened yourself up to receive more of what you need.

This lesson is not about judgment or being hard on yourself for what you think your failings or weaknesses are. Rather, it is about taking a step back, knowing everyone has their challenges and that with an earnest, heartfelt desire to change for the better, you can do it. The answer is not in a pill or a quick fix. The answer is in how deeply you can commit to yourself.

Once aware that you have patterns, you can change the ones you do not like. You will transform lower energies and lift yourself up in the process. This is what living fearlessly is all about. It is about reprogramming your mind and expanding your energetic frequency. You are clearing your old hard drive and downloading a new one. Super cool.

That is how it works. The moment you become aware of something, you can change it. You are not a victim, you are a creator. Own your patterns and begin to dispose of the ones that do not feel good to you. Simple.

1.4 Meditation Station

Some of you might have a regular meditation practice. If so, fantastic. Keep it up because it is important. For those of you who are brand new to meditation, best get started now. It is a must. Yes, a must.

Meditation will put you in touch with your core essence. If you are not meditating, that is totally cool, but here's the thing. If everything in your life was in perfect harmony, you probably wouldn't be reading this book, would you? So, meditation it is.

When I did Vipassana, a 10-day silent meditation course, I remember thinking that if the whole world could just sit down, shut up, and be still, all the world's problems would dissolve in an instant.

Meditation is one of the most powerful tools for personal transformation and although an ancient practice, it is more read-ily accessible than ever. The best way to start and stick to a meditation practice is to create a space for it. A special place, just for you.

In order to get to know yourself, you need to invest time in yourself. Even as little as 10 minutes a day can be a great start. You are establishing a new pattern that will help you become more aware of the ones you want to dissolve. See how that works?

The time you invest in yourself is a worthy endeavour. No one else can do this for you. Build your meditation station as a symbol of your own conscious transformational journey. It will be a friend and ally along the way.

What you need to do. Go shopping for some pretty things, or maybe some funky cool things to decorate your station. Let your unique preferences guide you to create a space with physical objects that represent the person you desire to become. Buy yourself a comfortable cushion to sit on, and maybe some snuggly blankets for the colder winter mornings depending on where you are in the world. Perhaps you will feel inspired to put up some inspirational pictures, paintings, or photographs that stimulate happy memories or future visions. Candles and crystals can be nice, too. Whatever your heart desires, do it, create it, and claim your space.

This is a sacred space that is just for you. Whether you know it or not, it will call to you. The very act of creating the station has established vibrational support for your daily practice.

Make your meditation station space inviting and beautiful. It is in this place that you are going to support, harness and bring forth the energies of your new life. Be proud of this space. Commit to the process and tell people, "Yeah, that is my meditation station. You should create one."

Morning Gratitude Meditation Practice

Sit in silence in your meditation station for a minimum of two minutes every morning. Set your alarm if you want to.

During this two minute practice, relax, focus on breathing deeply and steadily, and connect your awareness to the area of your heart. Repeat silently, 'I am love. I overflow with gratitude. I am love. I overflow with gratitude." This is only an example. Create your own mantra if you choose. Stay focussed on repeating these high-vibing words for the duration of your practice. Pay attention to how it makes you feel. If you feel calmer and more relaxed, job done.

If you do not, you need to sit longer and breathe deeper.

Oh, and have fun!

1.5 Beyond Words

The words we use carry a specific vibration like everything else. How you relate to the meaning of a word or group of words can affect how you feel. Pay close attention to the language you use and listen attentively to others. Make sure that when you are listening, you listen with your entire being, not just your ears. Notice if you can pick up a discord between what you say and how you feel, or what someone else is saying and how you feel.

As we move into greater awareness collectively, language changes to better reflect that change. Simply put, there are many words and expressions that no longer serve us because they are born out of separation. The words we use can either attract or repel a desired state.

For example, you may have watched or read some content on the Law of Attraction and are practicing really hard at manifesting money. However, you are still talking about how expensive things are. This is a block. Someone who is infinitely abundant would not talk about expense because they know they can afford anything they want. It is only through a belief in lack that an object can be expensive. In abundance, anything desired from an earnest, heartfelt place, is already yours. Expense does not come into it.

The reason it is important to pay attention to language is because we talk too much, not to mention, too quickly sometimes. As a society, we over analyse and go around in circles talking about all the problems and yet, never get quiet enough to uncover solutions. Quietness is your best friend when it comes to transforming your life.

As you become quiet and truly listen to yourself, and others, you consciously unravel patterns of behaviour that no longer help you. You needn't be hard on yourself or other people. You can quietly begin to reflect on how you speak to yourself and others. Be aware so you can catch people-pleasing patterns, which is saying things just to make someone feel better, or to go along with them. While you are doing this you might actually be feeding judgment and gossip. Notice how you talk about other people, and if you catch yourself speaking negatively about others, take note. Become more aware of the words you use that perpetuate an old world view of separation. Gossip is never a good thing, and despite being a difficult habit to break, should be avoided.

Spending time on your own and in silence helps you stay centred when it comes time to relate to other people. You can better notice the subtleties of language and the vibration of words. Quieting the mind actually helps you to refine your connection to your intuition. Anything you can do to practice paying attention and to interrupt the patterned thought stream in your mind is useful to you. Shift your focus away from judging. Notice and pay attention, ask yourself questions rather than making assumptions about things. Explore the meaning of words that you use and notice how they make you feel when you say them, or when others use them.

One word all too commonly used today is sorry. I hear people say it a lot, and for the most part, I am certain, they are not even aware they are saying it. Sorry comes from the word sorrow, and of despair. So, on a certain level, people who "apologise" all the time, whether they stepped in front of someone by accident, or were late for an appointment, are actually in despair and do not know it. They feel so bad about taking up space, about just being alive, that they are sorry for everything they do. And yes, it is a habit, but one worth becoming aware of so you can choose to use the word less, or at least, appropriately.

Being Step 1 you might be feeling kind of heavy, like "OMG, she's asking me to reinvent language?!?" Do not despair. It can be fun and inspire a huge amount of creativity. Language is always changing, and some changes are more enlightening and uplifting than others. Shakespeare anyone?

Again, there's nothing inherently wrong with the language we use, however, as our awareness expands, it extends naturally to what we mean by the words we use - how thoughtful our linguistic expression is. So, spend more time quietly listening and notice how often you just spurt stuff out without thinking. Resist the urge to fill the silence with words and see what happens.

Listen deeply always. Take notice. Be curious about words and thoughts and how they pertain to you. Question everything and remember it is not really about the words but your vibes in every moment. Get to know your vibes beyond the words and you will be onto something really beautiful.

You can do this. Have faith.

1.6 What To Expect

Expect to be significantly more aware of your emotional patterns; where, when and with whom you are triggered and with that, expect to sit through some emotional triggers, waves, and storms.

With your daily gratitude meditation practice, expect to feel calmer and more centred, especially regarding issues that used to worry you. If not quite there, you should be experiencing a sense of hope around your ability to overcome these challenges.

Emotional storms are intense, but once they pass, expect to feel relief. Expect to notice yourself reacting differently in situations.

Expect to notice language and communication in a different light.

Expect tears, which symbolise a breakthrough. You are moving up the vibrational scale and choosing a new way of living. Your tears are releasing years of burden, pain and guilt denied.

At this point, please be kind to yourself and others, be patient, reach out if you need to and trust that this inner work is the most important work you will ever do.

BONUS LESSON
Alternating Nostril Breathing

Alternating nostril breathing is a simple and effective technique that helps calm you as it balances the left and right sides of the brain, clearing your energetic pathways. In addition, it soothes your nervous system, supports your lungs, dissolves stress, relaxes the mind, and can help you fall asleep. It is a great breath practice to do before meditation or whenever your mind is super loud and chaotic. Within a minute of performing this breath technique you will feel more balanced and at ease. Try it out!

Sit in a comfortable position with a sense that your spine is gently lengthening. Relax your left arm. Place your right thumb on your right nostril and use your ring finger for your left nostril. You can gently relax or place your index and middle finger in between your eyebrows.

To begin, exhale completely and then use your thumb to block your right nostril. Inhale slowly and steadily through your left nostril and then, use your ring finger to block your left nostril and gently suspend your breath for a second or two. Release your thumb and exhale slowly and completely through your right nostril. Inhale through your right nostril, use your thumb to block your right nostril and suspend your breath. Release your ring finger and exhale slowly and completely through your left nostril. Continue to alternate. Feel free to play around with holding your breath momentarily at the top of the inhalation and establish a steady rhythmic pattern.

Pay attention to any imbalance in the strength and amount of air moving through each nostril. See if you can balance it through your own awareness.

Do this exercise whenever you are feeling stressed out and stick with it until you feel relief.

Step 1. Joy, Gratitude & Love

Exercise A.

When you are engaging with the mainstream media, i.e., watching a news report, or reading a headline in a newspaper, note how many times you feel the following three emotions and write them down. Was it anger? Write it down. Was it sadness? Write it down. Was it fear? Write it down. Do this every time you are triggered by a mainstream media channel.

This exercise demonstrates the conflict created by your interaction with mass media.

Exercise B.

Write down all the people that made you feel grateful to-day. At the end of the day stick it on your fridge or anywhere you can see it. Do this every day for a whole week. At the end of the week, take stock of names that repeat.

Exercise C.

When you wake up in the morning, write down the first thing you think with a brief description of how that thought makes you feel. Repeat for five days and be prepared to share fear-lessly with your tribe.

Exercise D.

The next time you are out with friends, abstain from alcohol for 30 minutes and observe how you feel. Be prepared to share your experience.

Exercise E.

Body image: Whenever you catch yourself feeling down about your body, notice it. Pay attention to the thoughts. Notice them. Instead of letting the thoughts run rampant. Say to your thoughts, 'I see you!' Call them out. And remind yourself that you are not here to judge yourself. Close your eyes, take a deep breath and imagine how you see yourself in the light, full of love and joy, powerful and radiant. Trust the image that arises as long as it makes you feel good. Hold this vision for a few seconds until you feel relief and calm. Then, give yourself a big hug and really mean it, love your body and be thankful to it. Do this every time you feel anxiety or stress around your body.

The opposite sex: Pay attention to what you think and say, along with what other people say about the opposite sex. Notice negative generalisations like, 'guys are so...', 'women are...' and so on. Recognise that this kind of language can create massive blocks. It categorises people and puts them into very limiting boxes and so creates a likewise limited scope for experience. In particular, pay attention to attacking the opposite sex in your mind by making it their fault for how you feel. If you notice you are angry, instead of attacking the opposite sex for how you feel, own your feelings. Withdraw from the situation and breathe deeply. Shine light on your feelings and begin imagining how you would like to feel. Is it more supported? Maybe it is more loved. Continue to breathe, imagine and sit until you genuinely feel clear and more positive regarding the person or situation. Do this every time you are triggered in a negative way.

Money: When you get a bill, notice how you feel. If you experience worry, notice it, feel into it, and flip it in the moment by choosing to practice gratitude instead. Be thankful for the fact that you have a home, with heat and electricity. Sit with the emotional charge, while breathing deeply and applying gratitude in the place of worry, until the worry shifts into relief and eventually calm. Then, pay your bill with love. Do this every time, with every worry and before you know it, you will have shifted your frequency around paying bills, and opened yourself up to receiving more of what you truly desire.

Exercise F.

Sit in silence in your meditation station for a minimum of two minutes every morning (you can set your alarm if you want to).

During this 2-minute practice, relax, focus on breathing deeply and steadily, and connect your awareness to the area of your heart. Repeat in your mind, "I am Love. I am overflowing with gratitude. I am Love. I am overflowing with gratitude." Be creative and feel free to explore your own gratitude mantra. Stay focussed on repeating the high-vibing words for the duration of your practice. Pay attention to how it makes you feel. If you feel calmer and more relaxed, job done. If you don't feel better, you need to sit for longer, breathe deeper and let go of whatever it is you think you need to do, unless it is an absolute emergency.

Exercise G.

How many times do you say, 'sorry' in a day? Be prepared to share your number.

Step 2. Judgment: The Block to Bliss

2.1 Listen: Catching Your Judgments

"Love is the absence of judgment." The Dalai Lama

Living a fearless life means dissolving all judgments against yourself and the world you perceive. A judgment is an opinion, a belief you have about what you think this reality is and your place in it. As the Dalai Lama expressed so simply, there is no room for judgment when you are truly in a loving state.

In very simple terms, judgment is resistance to change and a lot of people fear change. Change is inevitable and it is time to embrace it!

Judgments block your light and inherent loving power. They block your ability to visualise what is possible. We are all taught to judge, we are taught to be divisive, but we can unlearn this way of perceiving by diligently altering our own opinions and assumptions about who we are and what we are capable of as a collective consciousness.

Every time you judge your external reality, you are actually stating a thought you hold against yourself. You may judge a person's weight, or wealth. You might judge and criticise bankers and corporations. From the small to the big, judging is the same and it does not serve you. These judgments hold you back from expanding and raising your frequency. You are going to learn that loving everything, even the horror, the war, the poverty and everything you think is bad, is the way forward.

That which you judge, you push against. By doing so you place yourself in resistance and limit yourself and others. When you are in judgment mode, you feel contracted and heavy. We know all too well that people fight to protect their judgments because they believe their identity is interwoven with them. You are going to break free from this patterned thinking and acting and redefine who you think you are. You are going to create an inner world where judgment cannot survive.

I spent most of my life judging my body, so body image was a massive theme and challenge for me. My judgments against myself kept me in painful, self-loathing patterns for over twenty years. I was never good enough. I was ashamed and I felt guilty just for being hungry.

When I started to do this work, I finally heard my own judgmental thoughts against myself. "You are disgusting" I'd say while recoiling at the sight of myself in the mirror. Deep down, all I wanted was to feel beautiful, so I tried a different tactic.

I began with gentle reminders like "I am not here to judge myself", and practiced loving my body, even when I did not really feel it. I would hug myself and pretend I was applying bandages on my wounds, which were all over my entire body. I processed many emotional storms, and over time, I started to see a different reflection. Within two years of doing this inner work, my body transformed, not through will power or trying to manage my diet and exercise routines, but through unconditional love and honouring the person I imagined myself to be.

You can do the same thing.

Paying attention to how you think and feel is your gateway to freedom. The mind is very muddled with an array of judgments so this process requires profound commitment and fierce love. It is the love you carry in your heart, the desire for a peaceful world that will guide you all the way. Your judgments only limit you, so it is time to let them all go.

What are you healing through this practice? You are healing the conflict of separation, of "us against them" thinking. There is no force outside of you pulling you a part – unless you believe it. Once you recognise and own this way of thinking and being, your judgments will become more obvious to you. When you find yourself contracted or angry, pay attention to your thoughts because you are likely in attack or blame mode. Remember, attack and defence is the same energy. Whether you are defending or justifying your own behaviour, you are still attacking the external world, hence holding judgment and blocking your bliss.

Judgment leads to superiority and inferiority complexes. These distortions set people up to believe they are either better than others, or keep them feeling stuck in low vibes because they feel less than others. These reactions become an ego game that perpetuates limiting behaviour and as we know, painful patterns. Think of it like this. When you were little war was scary and you knew it did not make sense to you. Over time, as you were conditioned by media and the system, you came to rationalise its existence whilst fighting against it.

It might seem impossible to love something like war. You must remember that war represents the conflict of separation within us all and that your loving imagination has the power to transform war into something harmonious. Your love understands human frailty because it can feel it, the collective angst and turmoil that degrades life is caused by hatred and apathy, and it flows in you, too. You long to transform and expose all that limited and divisive behaviour to the radiant light of unconditional, fearless love. So without fear, you envision a world without war, you re-tell the old stories, and relinquish any judgment against war mongers, liars, haters, etc. The degree with which you can love it all, is the degree with which you can transform it.

I know it does not feel good right now. Taking responsibility for your part in the creation of it is hard. You must feel the pain of war and violence and then allow those difficult feelings to transform through love. It is the only way toward true and lasting peace.

Now that you have begun, you can no longer simply judge and turn away from the pain you feel. No longer can you remain silent in your heartache and in denial of your own attacks. Dissolve the hurt of the "us against them" mentality, and see a world of unity instead. See it with your inner eye and believe that it is possible.

We need each other more than ever to stand together in LOVE. No more are the rulers and the authorities going to laugh at love as a whimsical, frivolous emotion. Love is powerful, and the only answer. The love we feel is going to soften us and break us down and then build us up again, stronger than ever.

In the meantime, be patient. Notice the little and big judgments you carry and dissolve them all with loving awareness. There will be some heavy emotional storms possible here, but you are not alone. Keep reminding yourself of that, and know you are doing this for yourself and the whole big wonderful world.

2.2 Forgiveness

"If we really want to love, we must learn how to forgive." Mother Teresa

Forgiveness, why do we need it? Straight up, peeps who hold grudges and are unforgiving are really unhappy people. You want to be happy, right? Well, as you dissolve your judgments, forgiveness is the antidote.

When you are processing emotional density, the inner act of forgiving yourself and others, will assist you in the transforming process. You are responsible for all that you hold energetically speaking. In order to lighten those heavy emotions you need to consciously forgive the circumstances, and your role in the creation of them.

Forgiveness is a loving and compassionate act. Forgiveness is needed because of how messed up things are, in particular, with regards to judgments. Your judgments have been

52

hurting you and you have become accustomed to living in pain. As you shine the light of your awareness onto your judgments, forgiveness will soothe the pain.

Now then, remember in Step 1, we discussed 'beyond words'? This is relevant now because it is pretty easy to say, "Oh yeah, I forgive that person". Ah, but true forgiveness is not really about the other person, but rather, your initial judgment against someone, so forgiving creates an inner vibrational shift that un-blocks the judgment from your energetic being.

You can feel the accuracy of forgiveness by how unbur-dened you feel once you have released the judgment. If you still feel hard or rigid toward someone or a past situation, you have not fully forgiven. Continuing on, in order to unburden from re-grets, grudges and so on, you need to start forgiving everything and everyone in your life, including you.

It is highly likely there are specific people, past situations, and broader social issues that need your forgiveness. Perhaps you harshly judge other women for what they wear because you secretly wish you could wear a similar style. It may be that you are constantly attacking bankers because you blame them for your lack of financial stability. Maybe you secretly hate men be-cause of how your father treated you. The reality is, unless you forgive the past and everyone involved, you will unconsciously sabotage many of your endeavours because you are still blam-ing the external world for how you feel. Forgiveness changes everything and liberates you to create an abundant and loving fu-ture, even if it does not make sense to you right now.

Forgiveness is not a self-righteous act of superiority. It is something we do in our hearts. Every time you experience anger or sadness, it is partly you unable to forgive yourself for all the years that you have not been loving yourself, or for the years that you have been judging yourself and everybody around you. Wouldn't it be great if we did not need forgiveness anymore? Think about it, forgiveness is another human idea created as a way to heal judgments. If we stopped judging each other there would be no need for forgiveness. In the meantime, forgiveness is a great help when it comes to dissolving and working through emotional storms. Whenever you have an emotional storm you apply a salve to your wound of separation simply by asking yourself to be forgiven. You are allowed to forgive yourself. In fact, it is only ever you despite what you may have been led to believe.

Deep healing forgiveness does not come from someone outside of you. That distorted concept is perpetuated in religious institutions and is a disempowering teaching which enslaves people who remain bound by the fear of an almighty, judgmental force separate from them. There is nothing in this universe which is separate from you. We are, all of us, one with the highest of the high and the lowest of the low. We are sacred, divine, and beautifully able to forgive.

To live an empowered and enlightened life you have to be able to own up to the fact that you created your own experience, every situation and encounter was a choice on some level of your being, and everything you go through is you teaching yourself more about you. You are constantly creating, so be aware of the vibes you are putting out there. Straight up, if you are holding grievances, grudges, burdens, regret, you are actually creating more of the same. Is that what you want? Didn't think so. Forgiveness leads to freedom.

How to Forgive

You now know the work is inside you and requires your love, honesty, and fearlessness so within your heart, imagine a past situation in which you were hurt by someone and feel the pain associated with it. As you imagine, surround yourself and the other in light. You may cry tears of relief, you might have to scream out all your rage, but eventually, you will feel lighter and more peaceful. You will know you have let it go.

When you have truly forgiven, there is no longer an emotional charge when it comes to the person or situation you have forgiven. There is clarity, an honest love (which does not mean you have to hang out with that person), and energetically you have dissolved the density associated with your past grudge. Well done!

Next Level Forgiveness

Once you have done the "How to Forgive" exercise with all your past hurts and grievances, eventually you won't need it anymore because you will no longer be creating situations that require your forgiveness. Instead, you will be dissolving your emotional triggers before they become an embedded attack pattern, like holding a grudge. No more holding grudges, okay?

I am going to ask you now to forgive a bunch of stuff. Please forgive yourself for thinking somebody could hurt you without your permission. Forgive yourself for ever hating yourself, judging yourself, or judging this world as one of darkness. Forgive yourself for forgetting your radiant sacredness. Forgive yourself for ever thinking anyone could be unworthy, or poor, or greedy, or mean. Forgive it all.

Forgive yourself for every grievance, every grudge, every painful distortion and every unloving thought, for all your limiting beliefs and for every judgment. Continue to do this with every emotional trigger, and every time you think a nasty thought. Forgive yourself for it all, over and over again.

Your forgiveness liberates you and the world. Forgiveness restores your childlike innocence and curiosity and sense of wonder. Forgiveness is like a medicine that will help heal the wounds of the world. First, you must heal yourself, which means every time you notice a negative emotion, know there's a judgment. Maybe you are blaming something outside of yourself for how you feel. It is okay, simply own it, feel it and transform it with the help of forgiveness and unconditional love.

Remember: You can't force this stuff on other people. We can support, love, offer a helping hand. To truly change the world, leading with a fearless, loving example is the only way. It is not about words, or forcing your way onto another, it is simply about walking the walk.

2.3 Vulnerability

"To love is to be vulnerable." C.S. Lewis

To the distorted mind, vulnerability is perceived as a weakness or failure. What is vulnerability other than the ability to truly feel and if needed, express emotions? Vulnerability is honesty and openness. Your vulnerability opens a door to greater compassion and love for yourself and the world. Vulnerability softens you and breaks down your barriers, which then, softens and breaks down the barriers of the world around you. It is one way to elicit the ripple effect.

In the world of separation, or you could call it the world of attack and defence, it is obvious why vulnerability is deemed a weakness. When your guard is down, you are vulnerable, exposed to attack, and that is a scary thing. The need to be on guard is part of the illusion we are now asking ourselves to question. As we question, we begin to see that we must dismantle this concept in order to truly empower the individual, and subsequently the masses, into a higher and unified global perspective.

Part of the reason people are so afraid of vulnerability is because they have created a multitude of fearful barriers. The pain and hard lessons learned in a lifetime have shielded their hearts so any talk of love, they laugh or scoff at. They are far removed from that feeling. We can, and we must, begin to give permission to one another to not only feel, but to express what lies within.

Beyond our pain, anger and sadness, there is essential wisdom that has been hidden from our minds to the point of total forgetfulness. We cannot fully access or share this wisdom until we dispel long held beliefs around separation. Simply by engaging with this material, you have responded to your own desire for spiritual growth and personal transformation. You are forging a path toward greater unity within you and therefore, for all.

If you are not willing to be vulnerable, you are resisting change. Perhaps you are too afraid of what lies underneath the shields that have been protecting your heart. Here is where great compassion comes in. People resist change because they are in so much pain. Lifting the lid on their emotions and becoming vulnerable exposes every wound and that is a scary prospect. Sitting through intense emotional storms requires courage and for some, it is just too much to bear. You can help ease the collective pain by allowing your vulnerable-self to show the way.

Vulnerability can become your greatest strength. Gandhi and Martin Luther King were vulnerable leaders, wisdom teachers who taught non-violent resistance as a fundamental exercise for social change. It is time to unite and stand in this energy now, to be vulnerable so that you can access all the energy of fearless love. Be vulnerable so that you can access your wisdom, feel your depths, clear out that which weighs you down, and rise to higher heights of possibility.

As mentioned, in the old world of separation and attack, vulnerability is feared and so distorted into a weakness. You know better now. We can change our view, embrace vulnerability and move toward oneness.

As you redefine who you are with love, you also redefine the world's thinking. What was once seen as a weakness, becomes a strength.

In your vulnerability you become a truly compassionate and powerful leader for humanity.

Do it up y'all. You got this.

2.4 Allowing

Allowing is an aid to moving through your resistance to change. With vulnerability, allowing becomes much easier. When you allow life to unfold and simply be what it is, you create more space within yourself to own your judgments, practice forgiveness, and process the most challenging emotions you carry. If you are unable to allow something that shows up, there is a reason. It most likely means you are still judging something and are in denial. Being in a state of denial or judgment keeps your frequency low. Allowing helps you shift out of these states more quickly.

In order to make changes you need to allow yourself to be exactly as you are. Allow yourself in any moment to feel what you feel, to do what you do; good or bad. Allowing helps you see yourself more clearly. Allow your judgments, allow other people's behaviour, and allow the world to be what it is. Because, after all, it is what it is.

The reality is a lot of folks assume they know what is right for themselves and the rest of humanity, so much so that they limit their scope for a broader reality. If you are serious about making changes in your life, then allow everything to be totally what it is in any given moment. Even if you do not believe it is "right", or you think you need to keep trying to improve and be better, just allow it all. Recognise you can allow and not accept something at the same time. Allowing is like stepping back from the situation, withdrawing your attachment to the external and dropping into your silent awareness, so that you can chill out, re-arrange your perception, and imagine something which feels better.

This concept of allowing is a constant reminder for you to notice when you are angry, or jealous, to see the feeling and allow it so you can step back from it and eventually disengage from it completely. Let me elaborate.

You have been triggered and begin to feel angry. Instead of resisting or bottling the emotion, allow it to be there. Now that you have allowed yourself to be angry, you are better able to notice any judgmental thoughts that go along with the feeling, because you have dropped any resistance to the anger. You can stand back a bit and perceive the emotion, maybe have a chat with it. Anger is powerful after all and appreciates attention.

It may not always feel good when your emotions are trying to speak to you. They are telling you things you need to know or they wouldn't be there. As for anger, heck, we live in a world that perpetuates war. That is some serious anger issues stuff going on. You are working on transforming that anger with love. If we all did it, there would be no war.

If anytime along the way you find you are noticing your own mind's wacky attacking thoughts, fantastic! You are becoming more empowered by recognising you have them, rather than blindly jumping on the opinionated bandwagon of judgment. It is part of the process, especially when things start to get gritty. You may be dealing with a lot of anger, which when allowed to be there, can dissolve more quickly than if you deny it. Painful emotional storms can be processed when you learn to allow yourself to feel the fullness of who you are in any given moment.

Allowing gives you space to see your judgments; it makes space for you to change and it is like a bridge into acceptance. It is easy enough to say you accept this or that, but if secretly you are still holding judgments or blame, you cannot access true acceptance. Allowing is the next best thing. And remember, this is very subtle work. It might surprise you just how densely populated your mind is with assumptions, judgments, and limiting beliefs. Be kind to yourself. Apply lots of forgiveness, it will help.

When you are allowing, you are also not judging. When you allow yourself to be angry, or confused, or sad, whatever it is, there is less need to attack the external world for how you feel. Why? Because, you are giving yourself permission to allow all your feelings to be there, and so you naturally drop the need to defend against your own feelings, which is an attack on the external reality. Once you get this, you are well on your way to a more enlightened state.

Perhaps you have already experienced the shift that happens inside when you forgive yourself sincerely. Being in a state of allowing is similar to forgiveness. It does not mean you are complacent, however, you can always remove yourself from challenging situations. Simply continue to do the inner work until you can genuinely hold a loving frequency for the people or situations that once troubled you.

You have more than likely spent most of your life building up big walls which you think will protect you from that scary world out there. What you and the majority of humans have forgotten is that you are the creator of that scary world you see and now, you are choosing to create a different one. A world that is more loving and playful. To get there, you need to totally allow yourself to be where you are and own wherever that is, fearlessly.

Allow the world to be as it is. This allowing is an act of creating more space. You are doing the work by catching your judgments, and then forgiving yourself for that judgment. And now, you are stepping even further back and allowing this whole process to have its way with you. It is a miracle. You are allowed to allow, no matter what. Allow the totality of your expression to be exactly what it is, in any given moment.

By doing this work in your own life, you naturally give others permission to do the same. Your uniqueness shines like a beacon for others. It is pretty awesome stuff. If you can allow yourself to be wherever and whatever you are, you can then practice that with other people. The beauty of this is that when you get really, really good at just allowing everything to be, you are going to drop in to total unconditional acceptance of all of creation and that is one huge wow!

As you allow, you create more space. And that space is making room for more joy, more love, and peace.

2.5 Acceptance

"Happiness can exist only in acceptance." George Orwell

True acceptance is a state of non-judgment. Acceptance is our total commitment to, "I am what I am." Now, say that to yourself – "I am what I am." If you can accept yourself completely in any given moment, you are doing amazing work. Each step in this guide is a pillar for your new foundation. Each lesson serves to support and encourage you on your road to total transformation.

You have judgments, which are against yourself and the world. You are not the only one. By reading this book, and joining this community, you have empowered your ability to catch those judgments, to shine the light of your awareness onto them, and to forgive.

As you absorb and integrate the material, know that you will have your own very unique and special way of working with it. Trust your inner process. Transformation takes time, so be patient and just keep going. As the saying goes, "practice makes perfect".

You have been conditioned to judge and as you own and accept the part you played in creating those conditions, you are consciously choosing another way of perceiving. Now, you are choosing to alter conditions that do not feel good to you anymore and freeing yourself. Living in acceptance is pretty darn close to freedom.

A true state of unconditional acceptance will drastically shift your experiences. People may react differently towards you than they used to which only acts to highlight your own behaviour. Acceptance is neutral just like love. When you are having an experience, especially a challenging one, you can either judge it or accept it. Accepting it, sets you free. Judging it enslaves you. It is that simple.

As you practice allowing, you soften. Your vulnerability and increasing gentleness ushers you into acceptance. This is not about burying your head in the sand and denying how you feel, but rather owning how you feel and choosing to accept it rather than attack yourself or someone else for your feelings.

As you accept yourself, you can better accept the world, and thus, you can love it better. And I am pretty sure sweet Mother Earth would appreciate your love right about now. We all know how important it is to feel accepted. It is about connection and belonging. If you are here, you belong here, whether you believe it or not. By now, you know that if you feel something negative, it is in you and you can catch it, own it, forgive yourself, and transform it.

Change is inevitable. Resisting change only creates more pain. No matter what "the system" says, most of us can see quite clearly that a lot of what we have been doing is not working for us, we are spinning. Change is needed obviously and it starts, oddly, with acceptance. The more you can come into this space of total unconditional acceptance, the easier it will be to change.

Your ability to accept yourself is really your creative control with regards to how much you love your life. If you say, "No, not going to do it, can't accept myself." That is it, we're done here. I hope, however, you have not said that because this lesson is about you going right to the core of your being and saying to yourself, "No matter what, I am going to accept myself." No matter how ugly you might think your life looks, no matter how poor you might think you are, no matter how many things you have done that you feel totally ashamed of and totally guilty of, no matter what, you are going to accept it. Why? Because this whole world that we're all a part of needs accepting. You know it is true. Deep, deep down in your core you wouldn't be alive unless you accepted yourself.

I know I keep reminding you, but it is key that you realise you are the one who created your life and, therefore, you are the one who is going to transform it. Remind yourself of this – diligently - and, allow it. By allowing, you have cleared out some junk inside so accepting should come easier. You have tapped into your essential self, your creative life force and creation is an accepting force. It is very, very liberating, very freeing, very allowing.

Acceptance Affirmation: I am totally loved and accepted always. Apply this affirmation whenever you notice you are in judgment mode. You are amazing, accept yourself because you are beautiful. You really, really are.

2.6 What To Expect

Expect to become hyper-aware of how judgmental you are! Expect to continue sitting through some heavy emotional storms. The depth and weight of those emotions (which is about how traumatic the experience that created it is, and how long you have been carrying it with you) will dictate the intensity of your emotional storms.

Each of us is completely unique so experiences will differ from one person to the next. As long as you allow and remain detached and forgiving, you will survive them all and feel much lighter and clearer over time.

Some of you may experience radical change in your life after sitting through just one emotional storm, while others may need to sit through quite a few in order to begin to feel, and then see, real change in circumstances. Remember that this is in no way a quick fix programme. I'd be lying if I said it was going to take a month and then, poof, you are free. You need to learn patience, and be diligent in your commitment for change, in order for it to be lasting.

In times of distress, make sure you reach out. Although it is recommended to step away from people in order to process an emotional storm, be mindful of the temptation to isolate, as this could lead to wallowing in your emotions and fuelling self-pity. On the flip-side, avoid the temptation to escape your feelings with excessive partying. Again, you are never bad or wrong, just be aware and be willing to face your demons.

BONUS LESSON
Breath of Fire

Breath of fire is a really cool breathing technique practiced in yoga traditions. It is useful when you are feeling mega emotional. I have heard people use the expression, "drowning in emotion". Whenever you feel that way, this breathing exercise will help. You can do it anywhere, just be aware that people might look at you funny.

Breath of fire is a pumping action of your tummy, using your diaphragm and abdominal muscles to breathe rapidly through your nose. You are forcefully pushing out your exhalation by contracting your tummy muscles and alternatively relaxing your diaphragm to allow a passive inhalation.

In the beginning, take it slow so that your body can get used to it, and can maintain a steady, rhythmic, pumping action.

As you become familiar with the exercise, speed it up. It is always practiced through the nostrils with the mouth closed. It releases toxins and deposits from the lungs, expands the lung capacity, and increases vitality. Yay!

The fiery nature of this technique can burn up dense emotions and lift you out of your emotional watery depths.

Try it out for 30 seconds and see how you feel afterwards. Feel free to extend the length of your practice depending on how "watery" you feel. The longer you practice the more benefit you will feel. If you run out of breath, or feel light headed, stop, regroup and try again.

Step 2 - Judgment: The Block to Bliss

Exercise A.

Pick one judgment you make about yourself regularly. It can be as simple as saying "I hate my crooked tooth!" Or diminishing what you see as a lack of confidence with a comment like "Oh, silly me." Make a video, or if you prefer, write it down and be willing to share.

Exercise B.

With the judgment you highlighted from exercise A, now practice flipping it in your mind whenever it arises. For example, "I hate my crooked tooth", becomes "I love my crooked tooth". "Oh, silly me" becomes, "Oh, that's interesting" or "Oh, look at that". Play around until you find thought that feels lighter to you. Choose words and thoughts that empower you.

Exercise C.

You now know that the work is inside you and requires your love, honesty, and fearlessness. Go within your own heart and imagine a person that has brought you pain. Feel the burden. Now, imagine your heart surrounded with light. Extend that light as if it were a huge bubble to include the "other". You are now together in the bubble of light. Sit there and forgive. You may cry tears of relief, you might have to scream out all your rage, but eventually, you'll feel lighter. You will come to just know it is done.

When you have truly forgiven, there is no longer an emotional charge, i.e., "burden" when it comes to the person or situation you've forgiven. There is clarity and love felt (doesn't mean you have to hang out with that person) but energetically you have transformed the density associated with your grudges. And what remains is genuine love and compassion.

Take notes and be prepared to share your insights. This is an ongoing process.

Exercise D.

Where in your life are you afraid to be vulnerable? Write down 1-2 examples. Be prepared to share. And remember, vulnerability is innocence and an open heart, it's a beautiful thing and it's time you reclaim yours.

Exercise E.

Choose one thing that makes you angry or upsets you on a regular basis. Write it down. Challenge your perception by finding 2-3 examples of how you could practice allowing, while experiencing uncomfortable emotions. Be willing to share your experience.

Exercise F.

Practice with a trusted friend.

Person A says to person B: "You are loved and accepted always."

Person B responds: "Yes, I am loved and accepted always."

Notice any emotions that arise. Take note. Switch.

Continue relating your personal experiences in your journal.

Step 3. Getting to Know You: Self-study & Introspection

3.1 Intuition

"Have the courage to follow your heart and intuition. They some-how already know what you truly want to become." Steve Jobs

Intuition literally means 'inner teacher' or your inner guide. Some people call it a "gut feeling". Whatever you call it, we've all got one. For most of us, the mind is so loud and busy we let it distort or override inner guidance. And "the system" is really good at blocking people's connection too, hence the necessity of unplugging in order to re-attune to your essential frequency so you can listen, inwardly that is.

Your inner guide is always chillin'. The distorted mind blocks your chill-factor, while your intuition is so purely loving that it never ceases to remind you what is best for you. It tire-lessly and gently nudges you in the direction of your highest good. No matter what you say about it, or how often you choose another direction, it never gives up.

Your feelings reside mostly along the central channel of your body, from your gut to your throat, but as you know, you can have sensation anywhere in your body. The intuition is the "feeling" body, the emotional body, which is energy in motion, your energy in motion, which is, you. So, there is no separation between you and all that you feel. Your feelings are always com-municating with you, teaching. Getting to know your inner teacher is you getting to know a much wiser part of yourself, a deeper aspect as it were, and the part of you that is connected to Source, God, or All That Is.

Every single one of us has an intuitive sense. Your intuition is like all of the senses combined, working together in your favour. It is your guide to living the best life you can possibly live. Fortunately, there are many collective agreements around intuition which supports the fact that your intuition truly wants the best for you.

One thing that comes up when working with intuition and developing the skill of listening more diligently to its guidance is discernment, an intellectual, mental practice which assists people in determining the messages of the intuition. People can struggle between resistance and intuitive guidance. This will become clearer as you continue your transformation, and we will talk more about discernment later.

For now, recognise that becoming more intuitive goes hand in hand with dropping the hard edge of your judgments. Judgment blocks your bliss, remember, and your intuition wants you to experience bliss (if you desire it). So, if you are gripping onto your judgments, you won't be able to hear your intuition.

Your mind has formed patterns that take you into good feeling places and not good feeling places. When you feel awkward or uncomfortable with a thought or plan, it is often intuition trying to encourage you to look at another thought or a plan that is more aligned with your higher self.

Following your intuition does not always mean smooth sailing. It depends on where you are on your journey, on how much clearing needs to happen to get you from point A to wherever your next stop is. As you attune to your intuition and come to trust its guidance it will become easier to simply follow its direction. It always has your best interest at heart.

The "spiritual" path is avoided and/or stigmatised by the system because enlightenment is not thought attainable by the masses. It is also too scary, the idea of free-falling into emotions! With practice, however, it gets easier and easier, so that even painful emotions and challenging encounters can be processed and learned from with grace.

It is necessary to note that due to societal constructs being so deeply embedded in the collective memory against feeling feelings, and growing in awareness, strategies which encourage change can feel counterintuitive. Why? Your physical and emotional body is imprinted in such a way that makes you think this is how you are supposed to be, this is what you are supposed to do, or this is how we're all supposed to operate. As more minds awaken, the collective is realising that this just is not true. Uniformity numbs creativity and causes us to question our connection to our intuition, especially if it calls us to walk an unconventional path.

By consciously choosing to transform yourself, you are activating cells in your body which will help usher in enlightened, empowered thoughts. That is what innovation and inspiration is. If you recognise that a counterintuitive feeling is actually you breaking through deeply ingrained patterns, it can make it easier to allow change.

Getting to know your feelings without judgment is really helpful when it comes to picking up and fine tuning your connection to your intuition. Your intuition is soft, gentle, and nurturing. It might speak in whispers and subtle sensations when things are going good or in times of distress it will speak up loud and clear. Pay attention. Getting to know your intuition is a great start, but unless you follow through with your intuitive guidance, you won't see change. Unplug from uniformity and follow that feel good guidance. It (and the real you) wants you to shine your unique form of awesome onto everyone you meet and everything you encounter.

Again, with a conscious recognition of your inner teacher, you are committing further to owning the fact you are creating your life experience. The more you own it, the better life will get. Have fun with this! Do not be hard on yourself and enjoy getting to know your sensational body with a sense of curiosity, innocence, and an open mind. Your whole body is a divine, miraculous, and feeling being that is communicating with you continually about what resonates with you and what does not. Honour it all.

3.2 Distortion

A distortion is a change that makes something appear different than it is and it is usually unwanted. This whole reality is filled with distortions. The only way to shift them is to connect with source energy, or that which is your essential Self.

When things get bad in your life, when you feel hopeless or overwhelmed, it is a sign of how far away your distortions have taken you from your true purpose. Alignment is you in love with life. Out of alignment is you believing you have no power, no love. When you choose to live in love, you align with the highest frequencies of possibility, which unifies and serves to expand and uplift the entire planet, as opposed to the separate, fear-based distorted mind view, which separates and divides us.

Some people refer to the distorted mind as the ego, or fear mind. We are calling it the distorted mind because the term ego has been maligned a great deal in the last few years and there is nothing inherently wrong with the ego, or even fear, for that matter. They are words which describe an experiential reality that we have all agreed to create. The word 'ego', for example is just an idea, a part of your whole. It is not like there's some authoritative prison guard in your mind, sitting at a desk dictating your ego's projections. Nope, it is all you.

Too often, I observe people making excuses and blaming a certain behaviour on their ego. That is fine, but any excuse is a deflection of responsibility, an unwillingness to look at yourself honestly. Blaming your ego as if it were an external and uncontrollable entity, is no different than blaming your boss.

We can see the effects of extreme mental distortion all around us in corruption, deception, control, and domination. The trick is that you can actually choose to love all of it. There is no

76

moral judgment here. If you like manipulating and deceiving people, you can continue to do so, however as more minds shift into higher, loving frequencies, the harder it will be for you to maintain your distorted perceptions, because others will no longer want to play with you. Eventually, everyone is going to want to make the shift.

This transition, this awakening, this mission of raising the vibration of our own collective experience, is divine in nature. It is pre-agreed by many of us. All we need to do is get clear, allow, and accept. The rest will be revealed in perfect sequencing.

At this point, it is really important to remind yourself that everything is okay. Share your confidence with your family, friends, and co-workers. Be a soothing voice in these times of drastic change. Even when things appear to be getting bad or crazy chaotic, ground the higher energies into your loving heart and recognise the higher vibrational power you have to hold space for people.

At the same time, as you stay quiet and calm amidst the mess, do not hide. Do not remain silent when your intuition is guiding you to speak up. Do not remain still when you are being guided to take action.

You must own your distortions in order to change them. If you have a negative self-image, own it, and choose to see yourself as you desire to be, not what your distorted mind would have you think you are. That beautiful picture within your own mind is not a fantasy; it is actually your own divine blueprint. It is the higher vibrational version of who you are meant to become in this lifetime.

All of your dreams, all of your higher, glorious imaginings are yours to hold sacred. All you are doing daily is distinguishing between what resonates with you and what does not. You do not need anyone else's permission to align with what resonates with you, either. Clearing away distorted thinking and teachings will reinforce this.

The fact is, most of the people you are looking around at, and most of this world that we collectively create, is highly distorted. It is operating on layer upon convoluted layer. The more we expand, however, the more we expose and thus, the distortions appear and seem quite extreme. That is the point of doing this very important work. You are going inward to clear your fearful distortions and embody higher loving vibrations. The higher you go, the clearer you become. Soon, by your presence alone, you will shine a light on others' distortions bringing them into greater clarity without even saying a word. Powerful stuff.

Be proud of yourself as you unwrap your negative distorted views. It is not always easy. And it is not everyone's path. Feeling your way through this is hard work, but it is enlightening and totally epic at the same time.

The beauty is that the more conscious we become as a collective, the more fun all of this work can be. Until then, remember to be kind to yourself. You are a pioneer, building a bridge into a new, more harmonious reality.

Believe in yourself, and whenever you are in doubt, remember, I believe in you. I believe you can do this because I have directly experienced the transformative power of love.

3.3 Discernment

Discernment is the ability to grasp what is obscure. In a nutshell, it is the ability to tell the difference between what resonates with you and what does not. It is the refinement of your intellect on a higher level of awareness. Discernment is relevant when it comes to distinguishing between resistance and intuitive guidance, especially in the early stages of your transformation and specifically when it comes to taking new action-based direction.

We discussed in the intuition lesson, counterintuitive feeling. Society, the system, family, and institutions have programmed us quite effectively. Over time we establish what I like to call a default setting. This is your habitual pattern's set point. It is so persuasive that even if something is really awful for us, we will return to our default setting instead of facing something new that might be better.

For example, your intuition is asking you to leave a job. In one moment, you are inspired and feeling empowered and really believing you can change. The next day, you have a conversation with your spouse who reminds you that you have bills to pay and that you can't just leave your job because your intuition told you to. You drop back into your default setting, believing you are a powerless victim of circumstance.

Along the way, you are very likely to bounce back and forth, from high level inspiration to your lower frequency default setting.

A great practice for discerning what is the best choice for your highest good is to check in with your heart space. Take a few deep breaths, close your eyes if possible and ask yourself the question, "Should I do this? Should I do that?" Your intuitive guidance will feel lighter, more spacious, even exciting, while your default setting will feel contracted.

Trust your vibes and remind yourself that you do not need anyone's permission to change into the person you desire to be. It is your choice, not theirs, and they can either accept it and grow with you, or stay where they are. That is a free will thing. We will talk more about that later.

Pay attention. Be aware of the bouncing back and forth and be diligent with your commitment to love, abundance, and living your dreams. Keep going.

3.4 Stream Writing & Creative Expression

Creative expression is vital to your expansion; vital. Stream writing is a great and really easy way to tap into your creativity, especially if it has been shut down for a while. Stream writing is a way to get clear on what you are thinking about. It helps you to pay attention and further detach from thoughts.

When relaxed and quiet, you can tap into a level of intelligence otherwise blocked. Also, because most of us are programmed to respond in certain ways, it is a good way to practice unfiltered expression which just means you are expressing yourself honestly without judgment.

Most of us entered mainstream education at the young age of three or four and it had a deep impact on our energetic structure, hence the power the default setting has. Our trusting and innocent natures absorbed teachings and started believing we were limited. Authority figures including your parents told you over and over again, "No, you can't do it that way, you need to do it this way, or else." These teachings have a profound impact on how you relate to yourself. Now, it is time for you to break free and totally redefine what you can and cannot do according to your own resonance, not someone else's.

You have become accustomed to putting on different masks. You have been covering up to match others' expectations of you and before you know it, all those masks have covered up your own unique, creative sparkle. Your work from this point on is to remove all those masks and shine your radiant, loving essence onto your world.

Stream writing helps you do this because you are giving yourself permission to express yourself truly. No rules. No right or wrong, just you writing about your thoughts in any given moment.

There's no pressure here. What I do not want is for you to feel like this is another school assignment. All you need to do is put pen to paper or fingers to keyboard and write. If it is stressing you out, take a break. Creativity should not be stressful, that is a learned condition. True creativity is a fluid, timeless, effortless expression because it is coming from the infinite source of who you are, not the limited distortion of who you think you should be.

There's a whole bunch of multi-layered thoughts that can come up simply from being asked to write. You might notice a thought saying, "Who are you to be a writer? You are no good, you can't do that" or "I do not know what to write". Even if you end up repeating the same word over and over again, you are doing it!

Be aware that this is not a 'journal entry' where you tell your journal about your day. That is not what stream writing is. Stream writing is an unfiltered stream of consciousness, so drop the filters, stop trying, and let whatever is there come out. The main thing is that you are not writing a sentence and then going over it to double-check what you wrote. Ideally you are going to be writing a page or two pages and it just flows out. It might be total gobbledygook and not make any sense at all. Great, at least you have become aware of the total randomness of your own thought stream. With this kind of insight, you can be choosy with the thoughts you buy into.

Again, there is no judgment. It is just, "Hey, cool, look. That part of me makes no sense whatsoever." On the other hand, you might stream something beautiful, and inspirational. Keep your writings, they may inspire you later down the line.

If you feel blocked when it comes to writing, then try something different. Try painting, singing, dancing, or any free form of expression. But I recommend you come back to the writing.

There are infinite ways to explore your inner world. Every lesson in this guide strives to bring you back into yourself. Through stream writing, you can often access a divine wisdom that you might not have realised was there. All of us can access that part of ourselves, the place where infinite wisdom lives, we just need to keep believing and keep going.

What you write is for you. No one needs to read it. You are totally free to express yourself unfiltered, without judgment.

3.5 Divine Spark

Each and every one of us is a divine spark. It is our connection to everything and everyone. If the heart is closed due to painful past experiences, you need to open it again because that is where the divine spark lives. This may bring up emotions, but you are learning to sit and breathe through them. Be kind to yourself and know that by opening your heart you are inviting the creative spark that brought you here to shine. Trust that you are safe.

This concept can be challenging for us at varying times. When we are at a crossroads, for example, we can lose sight of the glow that is within us. The meditation below can help you keep your connection.

Daily Divine Spark Meditation Practice

Sitting comfortably in a quiet space, close your eyes and begin to focus on your breath. Breathe deeply into your seat and as you inhale, feel your breath moving up along your spine. As you exhale, gently maintain the length of your spine and allow the edges of your body to soften and relax. Begin to focus on the area of your heart. Feel into it. Breathe into it. Explore all the different areas and sensations within your heart. Be a witness to your experience.

Now begin to imagine a bright, sparkling white light emanating from your heart. Continue to focus on the breath and expand the light from within you.

Sit with this for at least 2 minutes every day.

This meditation can be very useful in times of distress or during an emotional storm. It helps open your heart and keep you clear and calm.

3.6 What To Expect

As long as you are following through with your intuitive guidance and transforming your emotional densities, your behavioural patterns will begin to morph. You may notice yourself gravitating to new people or spending more time alone, finding new activities while dropping others. Let yourself be guided to take action in ways that feel good to you and remember, it does not matter what other people think. Just be responsible for you and how you feel while respecting and honouring other people's free will.

It really is the little daily changes you make that deliver BIG changes in the long run. Your transformation may take a few months or years, but it will definitely happen as long as you keep going.

When you are having to sit with uncomfortable emotional sensations, remember this too shall pass. It always does. Have faith in the process and have faith in you.

Although you will be processing some deep emotional wounds, you are doing this work with others, which means you are never alone, even if it feels like it sometimes. Reaching out can take some practice, but it lightens your load and with a group of like minds, it is the best place to be. Be aware that some people in your life may not really get this stuff, which is totally cool, but it means they may not be the best support for you at this time. Try it out and if you notice yourself feeling bad, then definitely turn to The Fearless Life Tribe.

You do not need anyone's approval to do this work, only a genuine desire to expand and love your life. Others can choose the same when it is right for them.

Pay attention to signs. For example, you might go into a book store and notice a book that pops out at you. This means you are being guided to further your personal study. Buy the book and read it. It is likely to have information relevant to your journey. As you peel away your old walls, you will begin to see aspects of yourself that you could not see before. So, like the call to a new book, be open to all kinds of things. You might notice people on Facebook start to reach out to you, or you begin to have more inspired encounters with strangers. It is all part of it.

Just be aware that transformation is a total thing. You may just want to lose weight or make a little more money, but this work is an entire overhaul, so whatever you think the reason is for reading this book and exploring these thoughts, expect the unexpected. To the distorted logical mind, your anger has nothing to do with the extra weight you are carrying and yet, if you continue to transform your low frequency emotions with light and love, it is only a matter of time before the weight falls off, or the money shows up. The beauty is that this work is creating a new, more solid foundation for living a harmonious life. Everybody wins.

With every Step, expect to gain greater awareness, and greater mental focus.

You are doing so well. Give yourself a big round of applause, you deserve it.

BONUS LESSON
Guilt and Shame

Guilt and shame (G&S) run deep in the collective vibration. They are down there with the lowest of the low as far as frequency goes. The guilt and shame you carry is ultimately what sabotages your ability to genuinely enjoy life.

I am not going to harp on about certain religious ideas, but if you were taught about sin, which a lot of us were, it is likely you have guilt. And shame, too. They go hand in hand. How sweet. Except, not really.

G&S are really sticky emotions, like tar. Black, thick, messy, ugly and it gets everywhere. Your G&S are affecting pretty much every area of your life. You do not think you have G&S? You are either in denial or nearing the finish line to freedom. Bravo you, if the latter.

What I notice is that people feel guilty for just about everything. They feel guilty for resting, for eating, for taking a holiday, for making money, for partying, for having sex. The list is extensive. What is with the expression "guilty pleasure"? Why do we have to feel guilty when we are enjoying ourselves?

Reframe: You are not guilty for having a good time. You are not guilty for liking what you like. You are not guilty for having desires. You are free to be you in every moment, guilty or not. No strings attached. Guilt really has no place in the new world, so let's get rid of it, shall we? And how do you do this? You program a perpetual loop of reminders for yourself which affirm how much you deserve happiness, love, and abundance. This practice will gradually transform the G&S.

Question: Are you a people pleaser? If so, you have a lot of guilt. For women especially, people pleasing is a big one. Women are subliminally taught that if they are nice enough and pretty enough then they'll be looked after. It did not work for me. I tried it for a long time and ended up broke and alone. Why? Not because I wasn't pretty, and not because I wasn't nice. It was because my vibes were broke and alone. I was at my lowest, riddled with G&S because deep down I felt unworthy of being alive. All that people pleasing and trying to be pretty exhausted me; it used me up. How did I break free? I saw it, owned it, and transformed it, again and again.

I'll tell you right now, speaking your truth is definitely not people pleasing, far from it. In your new vibration, you will have to get comfortable with making people feel uncomfortable. Your light will illuminate people's darker sides, those bits of themselves they want to hide from. You will just have to accept that your role is to love, not please. You are no one's slave. You will no longer be manipulated. Your role now is to stay centred and make people feel good whenever you can and simply love. Leave the ones that attack you because they are still working through their own pain, but leave them with the light of your love.

Yes, G&S are huge, dense emotions to clear and break through as women. Of course, these lessons are not exclusive to women, men people please and carry G&S, too. We are all working toward balance and integration. But there are themes that are more gender specific.

The fellas have their own junk to work through. Like the, oh so obvious myth that "boys do not cry". I mean, what is that? They so do! Boys cry their vulnerable little eyes out just like girls do. Together, we need to take a deep breath and a good hard look at our world.

You have the power to transform all convention that feels limiting and then lead the way into more empowered and enlightened ways of living on this planet. How cool is that? While men feel guilty that they are not providing enough, women feel guilty that they just are not worthy, so nobody is winning. This is not good. We know denial does nothing but perpetuate the problem, so let's lift the lid on any problems and face them head on, fearlessly. It is the quickest way to transform. Let's feel the pain we have created without judgment and without blaming each other, so we can dissolve the energy that keeps us locked in destructive patterns.

Beware however. G&S is going to rise up from within you, like a thick black smoke-like fog as a backlash to you claiming your power. What?

You might decide to go on some really cool holiday because you have made extra cash this month and are feeling awesome. Suddenly, out of nowhere, you become overwhelmed with guilt. You are thinking to yourself, "I should not have spent that money. I should have put it into savings, like a responsible adult. I am such a twat. Stupid, bad girl!" Or, "Oh no, what will my parents think?!" Before you know it, you have a whole inner guilt dialogue going on. "How dare you? How dare you think you can break free from me? How dare you think you can actually be free, happy, and abundant?"

Right. Hold on and breathe. Now, see it. Recognise it for what it is. Transform it. It is okay and you are allowed to have a good time. You are allowed to spend money. And allowed to love your life.

See how there is a mind battle going on? There is an entire lesson on this later. Who is going to win? You can decide.

Realising your culpability in the state of the world is difficult – extremely so. Still, you must do it and face, head on, the aching human energy field. Then there's Earth. It is all like, "People, wake up! You are destroying me, your home!"

Until we take responsibility for our stupidity, we will continue to do really stupid stuff. One day we will laugh it off, but until that time comes, we must own up and forgive ourselves and shine forgiveness everywhere, including into our individual and collective guilt and shame which needs a loving hug, so it can be loved away once and for all.

Guilt also supports self-sabotage patterns. You might notice yourself sabotaging romantic love relationships, or your own healthy lifestyle routine. Anytime you are committing to making yourself feel better, the guilt energies will likely rise up and remind you that you do not deserve love, or health, so why bother.

G&S rises up thick and fast at the beginning. If you can sit through the experience and feel the ick-factor of G&S, you are well on your way. If you are still avoiding them or in denial, as mentioned, nothing will change and in fact, things can get worse. It is important to know that the only reason you ever feel bad about anything is because deep within you, somewhere, for some reason, you feel guilty and undeserving of love. Notice it. Own it. And choose to love yourself, no matter what.

Cry the tears you need to cry; feel the rage you need to feel; and remember this too shall pass.

When working with these dense emotions, try sweeping them into the area of your heart while you wait for them to transform. Let memories and sensations move through you and see them released. Recognise they have served a purpose in your life but that you do not need them anymore. Shine your light and keep breathing deeply until you feel better.

Remember: You are more powerful than guilt. Guilt is a dinky little creation you made up a long time ago. It is safe to let it go.

****

Imagine being in a maze. A big one. Suddenly, you feel lost. You are scared and stressed. You are running around looking for the way out and you just can't find it. Eventually, out of exhaustion, you collapse in a heap and fall asleep. When you wake up, you are looking down at your small, exhausted self, whispering "Get up." Your small self looks weary. You tell her, again, "Get up. Relax. Breathe. Walk straight ahead, then left." Small self stands up, eyes looking sceptical, but follows direction and steps forward a few paces before turning left. Suddenly, ta-da! Small self is free from the maze. How did she do it? With the help of higher self. Your higher self is always guiding you to freedom.

Trust in your inspiration and feel good vibes and be done with the guilt already!

P.S. You created the maze, too.

****

Facing and transforming guilt and shame means you will eventually stop punishing yourself. At that point, you will be a greater beacon for the world. It is a win for everyone.

You are amazing. Go ahead and explore your pleasure. Just do it. Your awesome life is on the other side of all your sticky icky G&S vibes. You got this.

Step 3. Getting to Know You

Exercise A.

Can you name 2 ways in which your inner teacher speaks to you? Explain. Be prepared to share your insights.

Exercise B.

Can you remember a time when you went against your 'gut' feeling or intuitive guidance? Explain how the circumstance unfolded and what the results were. Be prepared to share your experience.

Exercise C.

Choose 3 excuses you make or hear other people make on a regular basis. Write them down and be prepared to share your findings.

Exercise D.

Can you remember and list 1-2 instances you remained silent about when your intuition was asking you to speak up? Please describe.

Can you remember and list 1-2 instances you did not take action on when your intuition was asking you to? Please describe. Be prepared to share.

Exercise E.

Choose a moment when you must make a decision, for example, "Should I buy these shoes?" or "Should I go to that party?"

Once you have a question, close your eyes, take a deep breath and bring your awareness into the area of your heart. Feel into that space. Once you feel connected, ask yourself the question. The right answer will feel lighter and more open in your heart space, where the wrong answer will feel tighter and more contracted comparatively.

Write down your experience and any further questions that arise.

Be patient. Discernment is a practice and will develop over time.

Exercise F.

Spend 1-2 minutes a day this week stream writing. Make it a routine by choosing roughly the same time each day. Make this a part of your regular journal writing. This is just for you, but you are always welcome to share your concerns or ask any questions.

Exercise G.

Sitting comfortably in a quiet space, close your eyes and begin to focus on your breath. Breathe deeply into your seat and as you inhale, feel your breath moving up along your spine. As you exhale, gently maintain the length of your spine and allow

94

the edges of your body to soften and relax. Begin to focus on the area of your heart. Feel into it. Breathe into it. Explore all the different areas and sensations within your heart. Be a witness to your experience.

Now begin to imagine a bright, sparkling white light emanating from your heart. Continue to focus on the breath and expand the light from within you. Sit with this for at least 2 minutes every day.

This meditation can be very useful in times of distress or during an emotional storm. It is heart opening, clearing, and calming.

Step 4. Feeling Good

4.1 Feel Good Permission Slip

Permission yourself to feel good. Do not rely on other people to do this for you. Let's be honest, there is a lot of anger and misery in the world which is actually why you are here, consciously choosing to love your life. You desire change in a big way, and all change starts in you. So, you have to give yourself permission to be joyful and fulfilled, healthy and empowered. Be aware that your transformational journey, which is essentially an increase in the love and light energy, may trigger people. They might verbally attack you and challenge you during this process. Why does this happen? Well, your light is illuminating their dense energy, and if they are unaware or resistant to change, they will push against you and blame you for making them feel uncomfortable. It is not you. Love them and be willing to walk away. They will make the change when they are ready and desiring to do so.

Know that it is also you challenging, or testing, yourself when these encounters occur. Be aware that people might deny you and even go so far as to pick a fight with you. Be aware and responsible, diligent and committed to the process. You will get through this. Keep the faith.

I know that a large part of your journey up to this point may have taught you that life is hard and unfair, but it does not have to be. You are changing the delusion of misery by taking responsibility for all the years you bought into it, all the years you perpetuated the painful human story of control and domination. You are consciously transforming lower frequency energy patterns, which includes all your judgments, grudges, and grievances held against yourself and all other people, situations, events, institutions, and the world. In so doing, you are re-writing history and dissolving collective pain. It is true.

Because this work can be super intense, you must continually permission yourself to feel good and remind yourself that you are transforming your life, which requires perseverance. Remind yourself of the rewards love brings, and of the abundance that awaits you on the other side of your own breakthroughs. That is what you are doing, breaking through your old and limiting beliefs so that you can rise into freedom.

Due to dense energy patterns that exist in this world, yours included, you cannot be reliant on other people to show you exactly how, or give you permission to, love your life. You alone are responsible for your joy and fulfilment. Expecting other people to fulfil you is an old story and it is time to write a new one.

Throughout the process of transforming, pay close attention to people or environments that drain you. Feeling drained does not feel good. Again, it is your responsibility to remove yourself if this is happening, not out of judgment, but out of love for yourself. If you continue to engage in situations that drain you, and then complain about being drained, you are not being responsible. No excuses. If you notice the drainage, get out. You can always send mega love vibes to the person or situation that you are choosing to disengage from. And who knows, your departure from their life might end up inspiring them to make some changes. Do not worry either way, however. Their journey is their own, and if you sincerely hold them in love and light, they have a great chance of expanding.

On the flip side, pay attention to new people coming into your life. Now that you have been cleaning up your vibration, be open to "random stranger" encounters. You might bump into people in the street and start talking about how awesome meditation is, for example, or meet someone and before you know it, they are telling you their life story. You are both buzzing and you invite them to read this book with you. Who knows? Most importantly, stay open to new experiences and be willing to share more of who you are with the world.

Remember that it is your duty to feel good. You are on a mission here to uplift humanity and spread love and joy into the world. You cannot do that if you are complaining, un-feeling, and not owning your whole being. Once again, it is not about denial, rather it is about being aware of your energy vibrations. If you are dissolving a dense energy, you are detached from it and not in denial of it. There is a difference. You could say, "Oh gosh, there's some sadness" or, "Here is some pain" or, "I am really aware of feeling jealousy right now". You can own the lower vibes and all their darkness, but you do not need to buy into them anymore. You simply recognise them, sit with the feeling as long as you need to, breathe through them, and say, "I see you (insert crappy feeling here). Thank you, but I am ready to let you go now because I no longer believe you are useful to me or humanity. Bye-bye!" This is a practice, right? You have heard it before, practice makes perfect.

As you enlighten, you will become brighter. You will become lighter. Your light serves as a beacon for others who are seeking their own light. They will naturally gravitate towards you. It is magnetism. Really, it is the law of attraction, a natural and scientific way of comprehending how this reality works. When you expand your awareness beyond the day-to-day grind, you begin to remember why you are actually here. You are here to enjoy life.

Be really aware of holding yourself in a place of love and giving yourself the space you need to feel good. Permission yourself to disengage from any interactions that support separation and division, complaining, blaming, judging, or gossiping. In order to feel genuinely in love with your life, you must disengage from those frequencies and align with unity, empowerment, and love.

"With great power comes great responsibility." Uncle Ben from Spider-Man

As you become more responsible, you will become more powerful. Own your power. Be loving and compassionate. Feel good and rise with a clear voice for awesome change. See the world as you desire it to be, not what you were told it is. Use the love in your heart and your high-vibing imagination to create a world where everyone is safe, loved, and inspired. There is infinite abundance for all if we can just believe it to be so. Let us be responsible and aware of holding all of humanity in the light of love that transforms wounds into superpowers.

You are here to make a difference, because you can feel it and see it. Give yourself permission to own it and move with it. Do not let anyone bring you down or distract from your feel good mission. Choose to be of service to your brothers and sisters here and tell them that they too deserve to feel good. Lead by example, not by force.

Share that feel good permission slip with everyone you meet. Smile. Be kind. Be generous, but most of all, be YOU.

4.2 Loneliness

Loneliness is an effect of separation. Emotionally, loneliness is experienced as an unfulfilled desire for another person's company. At its worst, it can bring about a resignation to living a life without love and connection. Loneliness befalls someone who has given up hope. No one deserves to feel lonely, and yet, through the pain of separation, we isolate ourselves and fear connection. There is a difference between being alone and feeling loneliness. A feeling of loneliness is created via the belief that one is separate and alone in the world.

There is an expression, and I used to say it a lot when I was in despair, that "We live and die alone". And while it would appear to be the case, viewed from a perspective of unity and oneness, you could say that we live and die as one.

Spiritual awakening reminds us of our inherent connectedness. As we become more aware of this and embody the reality of oneness, we strengthen our connection. Therefore, even when we are alone, we needn't experience loneliness, because we know without doubt we are all connected. Your job is to be aware of feeling lonely because it needn't be a part of the process. However, like all emotions, make sure you let yourself feel, own, and transform it should it arise.

The fact is, a person can feel lonely in the middle of a crowded room. So much of the pain we harbour is rooted in this "live and die alone" belief. People desperately hold on to painful relationships because of a fear of loneliness. If you want to be truly free, you must change your perspective around what being alone means.

Throughout this process you are being asked to create more alone time for yourself so you can face this fear. Challenge your default setting and resist the urge to always make contact with people when you get itchy feet being alone in your own company. There are many ways to ignite the feeling of connectedness, from meditation to watching the stars at night.

****

One of my earliest spiritual awakenings happened at a time in my life when I was desperately unhappy and felt completely alien to the people around me. It was my first year at the University of British Columbia in Vancouver, Canada, after being sold the idea that university was going to be the best time of my life. It was not in my case. I made no friends and hid in my dorm room most of the time.

The campus was on the coast, and I often found myself taking long walks alone. One day, I was watching a sunset and without warning was overwhelmed with tears. In that moment I knew I was one with the sun and the sky. It brought me so much comfort at a time when I felt lonely and isolated.

****

It is my sincerest wish that no one in the world ever experience loneliness, alienation or a sense of un-belonging. There is no need for it, which is why this guidebook exists, my friends, to put an end to loneliness once and for all and to let unity and connectedness rise among humanity. And, for this reason, you must spend more time alone in order to face your fear of loneliness and transform it with love.

People still talk about spirituality in defined terms. Only priests or nuns are spiritual, for example. This is not true. We are all spiritual. Some just recognise their divine connected essence, while others deny it. The system would have you believe that you can't be spiritual unless you talk in whispers, never party, and renounce material goodies. This is just not true. The brokers on Wall Street are just as spiritual as the monks who meditate all day. The two simply have a different life path.

From the perspective of separation, spirituality is separate from who you are, hence it is all about what you do. From the perspective of oneness, everyone is spiritual, everyone belongs, and everyone is doing their thing with their own unique set of challenges and desires. There is no right way to be spiritual, because you are all already spirit which took form. Rather than trying to be spiritual, be fully alive. Awaken to your own aliveness and grab it. Face every fear, look into the darkest corners of your mind and feel your heartbeat, feel your breath, feel the life force coursing through you. Watch sunsets, observe birds and bees flying through the sky, trees swaying in the wind. Allow yourself to be moved by the grace of this planet. Find companionship, not just in other people, but in the world around you.

If you fear loneliness, dissolving it will be a massive shift for you. You can finally bridge into a new way of being because you have allowed yourself to feel into your higher, connected self. You can now experience the joy that comes when the fear of being alone goes away. Who knew being alone could be so great? You do not always have to choose to be alone, however.

When you have had enough of hanging on your own, reach out or call a friend. Ask the universe for more like-minded friends, write a message to The Fearless Life Tribe. Sit with your aloneness knowing that any feelings of loneliness will eventually pass because, after all, you are never alone.

Be proud of yourself for doing this important work and continue to shine especially for those who have been shunned by society. Be kind and giving to the homeless that you see. Give people your time, listen to them. Love them. It is your duty now more than ever. The world of isolation and fear dissolves when faced with togetherness and loving kindness.

Have faith with this one. Loneliness is a biggie. You need to break through its discomfort to rise above it. Eventually you can enjoy solitude. There may even come a time, when you crave it.

4.3 Repetition and Momentum

I have mentioned the adage, practice makes perfect. What is practice, really? It is repetition. You have been thinking and acting in certain ways, repeatedly, your entire life. Now you are at a point where much of what you have been thinking and doing does not feel good to you anymore, you are tired of it, and want to change. You are not going to initiate new patterns over-night, although nothing is impossible. Some of you might move fast while others move more slowly. My wish for you is that it does not take fifteen years, like it did for me, however, the time does not matter. You will learn, alter, and redefine yourself on your own terms. In fact, all of us are always adjusting, tweaking, and growing. It is not a quick fix this enlightenment thing despite what some might have you believe.

The system enjoys selling quick fixes, and everybody wants one. A pill, a 21-day program, the diet to end all diets, you name it. People are so desperate to be happy that they will pay anything to "fix" their problems. Yet, there is nothing out there that is ultimately going to fix you. You are going to fix yourself by becoming more aware, cleaning up your vibration, and owning the energy you are carrying. Simple enough, but not that easy, especially when you are getting started.

If you are unravelling patterns, you will not likely be finished after successfully sitting through one emotional storm. They tend to keep coming, and they will as long as you are challenging yourself. The good thing is that with faith and continued practice, you will see positive changes. You just have to keep at it, and you have to keep believing in the process. If you give up and decide that this is all hogwash, your world will stay the same. You will go back to telling the same old stories, blaming this, and complaining about that, whilst perpetuating the same old painful patterns. That is okay. You have free will. If, however, you desire real change in the world, that change has to start with you.

Developing a new way of being is no small task. You have to repeat the new practices you are being introduced to daily so you can truly feel what resonates with your higher self. The good news is that it does get easier. Of course it does. It must! This is where momentum comes in.

Physics defines momentum as "the quantity of motion of a moving body, measured as a product of its mass and velocity". Simply stated it means if you are moving, you have got momentum. Now, consider that definition in terms of raising your vibration. The more you move, or transform, your lower frequencies, the more frequency you can move because you are gaining momentum. How does this apply to practice? As you continue to faithfully practice, or "move", you are consciously building the momentum you need to move you from one point to another point. This guide helps build momentum even faster, and with even greater force, because there is a group pushing toward a similar point.

Earlier, when writing about vulnerability, I referred to the ripple effect which is a lovely image of the endless wave. You can also visualise a snowball getting bigger and bigger as it rolls down a hill. Either way, both images show what is happening when momentum builds. You are creating a whole new way of being and with even the slightest change, as long as you keep changing, you are building momentum for yourself and the collective, so keep it up!

Despite successes, there may be times when you wish you could turn back - climb out of the rabbit hole as it were. Thing is, once begun, we cannot go back because "back" does not exist anymore. You have changed. It is that simple. You can slow down, even stop for a time, but you cannot go back.

The time for great change has come and it is happening to us whether we like it or not. Simply put, you can resist all you like, which is only going to make your problems worse; or make the shift, which requires facing all your darkness. A reward of inner peace and freedom awaits if you decide to keep on going.

I often have moments where I want to say to the people of this world, "Hey, it is all good, no one's to blame for all the craziness, just stop focussing on it and come over here, where it is super fun and loving." The coolest thing about loving fearlessly is that regardless of what other people choose to do, you are going to love 'em anyway.

Have you been hiding from some dreams you have had since you were young? It seems a normal thing for many of us because we take on other people's limiting beliefs about life, and push our dreams away. Those dreams do not want to be forgotten, though, and as you clear and make space within your mind and body, be aware of them. They might just bubble up to the surface again. They are part of you still. It is also a fantastic sign that you are gaining momentum, so pay attention to those burning desires resurfacing. They are meant to.

Maybe you dreamt of working with animals, or developing new technology. Maybe you have a desire to be an artist and to live in a cabin by the sea. There is no right or wrong when it comes to your innocent dreams. They are what you are here to create, and the vision you were born with for your life shows them to you. Be courageous and reclaim them.

When it comes to your high-vibing dreams, repeat to yourself, "I can have that." Mean it. Now, say it again. "I can have that." Yes, you can!

Be aware that in spite of your new determination to live out an old dream, doubters might well show up as a reflection of your own self-doubt. You will hear things like, "Uh-uh, no you can't. Who do you think you are to dream big?" Hold fast. Do not waiver. Smile at the doubters, send them love, and walk away more deeply committed to your true nature than ever.

This is where repeated practice shows exponential growth; the more you do it, the easier it gets. Makes perfect sense. You are going to repeat, repeat, and repeat this work until it is your habit.

Stay strong. Keep believing with every cell of your being that your dreams are yours for the making. Keep going. Keep going. Just keep going. I am dreaming big for you.

4.4 Purposeful Break

You have been doing amazing work up to this point, so congratulations. Now, it is time for a purposeful break. You are going to reward yourself simply because you can.

Blinded by the system's inculcation, people believe they must work really hard, or achieve something great like a promotion, in order to deserve a break. Many believe that if they work hard enough, one day, near the end of their lives, they'll be able to rest and play. But that day never really comes, or it comes at a stage in life when the body is tired.

With that written, it is our heartfelt duty to honour and be grateful for all the hard work that has been done by people on this Earth. It all has relevance and adds meaning to our exist-ence. For many, working nine to five, serving family and their community in their own special way, is a valuable and honoura-ble service. This pattern of behaviour, however, limits potential and stifles an expanding human population. We need to become more creative around the idea of "work".

Ideally, in order to break cycles of poverty, routine, and boredom, the planet needs more entrepreneurial and innovative spirits. There should be no judgment around people who are still having a great time in the system as it is, but if you are not enjoy-ing your life, you are not adding as much value as possible. You are limiting your potential, and thus, limiting the potential for the entire human race. This is why you need to take a break.

Taking a break has a tendency to shift our mind-set and give us a slightly different perspective on our lives. The freedom we feel when we are on holiday shows us what we are capable of.

Somewhere along the way, millions of us threw away our sense of fun and wonderment. We bought into the grind of adult-hood with its toil and weight. We feared not having enough and got greedy. Ultimately, we ended up making choices that threaten our home and, therefore, our very existence. Seriously, in what universe does depleting resources needed to sustain life, make sense? However, what has this got to do with taking a pur-poseful break? It offers you the opportunity to look at your day-to-day existence from a different vantage point, and to relate to everything from a refreshed perspective. Straight up, the way we live in this current system of ours is super heavy and serious. In order to lighten up, you need to have more fun.

A purposeful break can be anything that brings back that childish enthusiasm for life. Go camping, take a weekend trip somewhere you have never been before. Go alone, or with good company, people you love hanging out with, who make you laugh and around whom you can be yourself. Maybe a getaway with your new tribe is in order? Most importantly, when it comes to planning a break, follow your feel good flow. Imagine something that would be really fun and then, go do it.

The reason for this is that you have to get used to having more fun and enjoying life in the simplest of ways. Spending time in nature and with people you love is the ultimate reward. Relish it. It is also a great way to decompress and to lighten up the process of change you are undergoing. Having fun is a way to get out of your head. If you decide to go camping, pay attention to nature. Feel it. Breathe with it. Take a juicy novel with you or even some ad-free entertainment, and switch off from yourself. The lighter you can be around this inner work, the easier and more fluid it becomes. You will see greater change if you take regular breaks from your 'normal' life.

This lesson might trigger you. You might feel guilty, or rationalise yourself out of taking a break. You might come up with excuses. "I am too busy. I have no time." That is resistance and you know how to put it in its place now, so do that and schedule your purposeful break ASAP.

In mainstream education, the workforce, organised religions and even many "spiritual" communities become rigid and dogmatic about their message. Despite this being a structured guide, there are no real rules. This is all about you remembering your essential self, the part of you that came here to enjoy life and experience LOVE. Bending structures and rule breaking is encouraged!

Later, we will talk about living in the flow. The advantage of playtime is that it helps establish and strengthen your flow state. Your service to the world will come from this place. The world as you have come to know it is an over-structured mess. You have to soften enough so you can melt that inflexibility. Rigidity supports resistance so we see even more rigid responses to change.

You are going to change that by becoming as flexible as possible, and by seeing beyond the rigid walls of the old paradigm. You are going to let yourself chill more, take duvet days, and book pampering weekends with the girls. Others might want to climb mountains, or deep sea dive. The form of your desired break time does not matter. Do things that represent relaxation and self-love. These actions, as long as they feel good to you, will assist in raising your vibration.

Booking a purposeful break is also an opportunity to show yourself how far you have come. Play as if your world is perfectly balanced and awesome. When you take your break, pretend you are living in bliss, in your version of paradise. Treat yourself and live in your imagination. Feel what it feels like. Try something new or do something differently than you usually do. Whatever you do, have fun.

The sky's the limit here. Take a purposeful break, claim your power in this lesson and follow through with the vision that feels most awesome to you. Enjoy your break. I'll see you on the other side!

4.5 What To Expect

With each Step, you are grounding more deeply into your new foundation and gaining clarity with every successful emotional transformation. It might still be heavy going, emotionally speaking, but you should feel relief at being supported through the process. You should also see some of the positive effects of practicing gratitude and acceptance on a daily basis.

As you continue to discern what your intuitive guidance is telling you, expect to notice more courage within. Expect an increase in your energy level. Notice how you are expecting good things to come and how some major challenges begin to be less challenging. Work related stress patterns are less stressful, for example. Overall, you should be feeling more confident and loving. You might experience moments of bliss or overwhelming gratitude to the point of tears. These are tears of joy. Know that moments of pleasure and happiness will come and go, but the underlying calm and serenity that is Love, will remain a constant.

At this stage, you might feel a new life direction is calling. Let yourself feel excited about this. If you are inclined to volunteer or help a friend, do it. Perhaps it is time to write a blog, or start vlogging. You needn't publicise these projects unless you want to, but your desire to share more of who you are becoming is part of the process. Do not shy away from what your inner guidance is asking of you.

If you are remembering dreams you once held, expect them to keep nudging you. Your heartfelt dreams are aligned with your purpose. If they are coming back to you, then fearlessly own them and harness a belief in them. Some of you may be called to teach, inspire, or share. You needn't wait for anyone's permission to do this. Start a class or set up a workshop. If you have a desire to help people by sharing your wisdom, then do it. Do it from an unconditional loving place, not an arrogant "I know what is best for people" place. Not that you would. Please follow through, even if it feels a little scary.

Along with all the goodies showing up, you may notice other things falling away, like certain people. It is okay. Let them go. Just like everything else in this transient reality, people come in and out of our lives to teach us things. If a relationship is hurting you, deal with the hurt, then forgive and release the person with love. Bear in mind, nothing is ever lost. Energy only changes, so hold people in the light of your love, but trust your intuition. If it is telling you to let go of people that are no longer in alignment with your resonance, then let them go.

As you continue to raise your vibration, you will notice a shift in how you communicate and listen to people. These are all signs that you are on the right track.

If you experience no changes at all, you either have more emotional storms to sit through, are being impatient, or this path is not right for you at this time. You are awesome no matter what.

Do not forget to share your stories and revelations. Your journey matters and it is time to share it.

BONUS LESSON
Conscious Movement

Conscious movement occurs when you pay attention to your breath and body as you move through space. When it comes to doing your inner work, you need to start paying attention to your thoughts and your body, because they are inseparable; they are one thing. In order to aid your expanding awareness, you must nurture and care for your body in a deeply loving and enjoyable way. This means moving around every day, and taking plenty of rest when you need to.

The system has imposed horrid, anti-body rules from the repetitive movement requirements in factories to being seated all day in an office environment. Fears and worries of all kinds have people stressed out, frazzling the body's nervous system and depleting the immune system. No wonder so many people are sick! Your body is not a machine. Instead, it is an ever evolving, fluid, vibrational organism, designed to move and function optimally when it is relaxed.

Collectively, we know that movement is vital for a healthy body. In the distorted world view, our bodies have become like an enemy, something to be hated or feared. There is a classic saying in the world of fitness. "No pain, no gain." It encourages suffering in order to maximise the body's potential. This may work for some, but if the pain is too painful, it is not worth the gain.

The body I desired manifested when I learned to love and honour my own unique needs. Simply put, if you are judging your body or feel you have to manage your body, you are not truly loving it. You need to love and accept your body totally and un-conditionally, and from this point onward, choose to move it in ways that feel enjoyable to you.

You can enjoy exercise and movement, and it does not need to be painful in order for you to achieve your ideal form. In fact, your ideal form will show itself when you truly love every cell of your being and honour your body's needs. There is no one right way to exercise, it all comes down to you and how you feel about your body. When you unconditionally love yourself, you will be guided to a movement practice that suits you and is per-fect for your perfect body.

****

Yoga is an ancient practice that recognises the inherent oneness of all life. It traditionally has eight steps, the third of which is movement. In yoga, movement is necessary to form a clear and aligned perception.

As a yoga guide and practitioner for nearly twenty years, I am a massive fan of the practice. However, I am all about helping you make yoga your own, and not getting too caught up in tradition and what other people claim yoga is. There is no right or wrong way to move, you just have to remain aware of your body, breathe deeply, and move in lots of different directions. You can flow around, play, and feel into the space that is your body. This will sensitise you to your body and increase your awareness and vitality.

As you become more aware of it, listen to your body and dialogue with it. I know that might sound super weird, but your body is you and if you are denying your body's needs, then you are denying you. Do not deny yourself, love yourself!

Keep going!

Step 4. Feeling Good

Exercise A.

Reflect for moment and remember a time when you felt someone let you down. Imagine the situation clearly and own all the feelings. Now, re-imagine the situation so that you did not feel let down. Keep at it until you feel better. This exercise can be repeated with all painful past experiences and memories.

Write down any insights and be prepared to share.

Exercise B.

Challenge your default setting and resist the urge to make contact with people when you get itchy feet being alone in your own company. When the urge arises, instead of giving into the lonely itch to contact someone, write down the time of day and make note of the sensations that arise. Be prepared to share.

Exercise C.

Create a vision board. Choose pictures and words that inspire you, and pin them onto a board. Put it where you can see it every day, perhaps close to your meditation station. Feel free to change, add to and re-do it whenever you want. This is an ongoing creative task. Be prepared to share your dreams with the others seeking a fearless life.

Exercise D.

Make a few notes about what this lesson brought up for you, both in the planning of the break and living it. Be prepared to share your experience.

Step 5. Surrender Knowing

5.1 Why Surrender?

"True love is an act of total surrender." Paulo Coelho

Like vulnerability, in the world of separation, surrender has a meaning associated with weakness. For example, when an army surrenders, they've lost the battle, and losing a fight is a failure when you are perceiving through the eyes of separation. By reversing the world's thinking you are no longer playing the game of war so not enforcing the "us against them" scenario. The word surrender can then take on a new meaning. Instead of seeing it as a weakness, you allow it to become a strength while you learn to play by the rules of love and unity. Indeed, surrender is a giving up, a yielding or submission. It also means to cease resistance. In the game of war, one ceases resistance to the enemy. In the game of life, one ceases resistance to love and compassion.

In order to expand your lightness and all those loving vibrations, you must surrender your life to Divine Law, over and over again. (By Divine Law, I mean the laws of the Universe, not man-made laws.) In the deepest way possible, you are surrendering everything you think you know and opening yourself up to a life beyond the one you currently see. Yes, it will feel scary, but your dream life is on the other side of all your fears. You must face them, surrender, and then, move far beyond them.

One day, you will find it hard to believe you used to be so wrapped up in the world of fear and separation. Until then, you will continue to unlearn what does not resonate with you and re-build anew from a loving perspective.

So, why are you being asked to surrender knowing? Simply put, we humans just do not really know anything for certain. The great mystery of life eludes us yet we go around pretending as if we know exactly what we're doing. Just like judgments block your bliss, knowing, or rather thinking you know something, is a potential block to your enlightenment.

As discussed, distorted ideas and thoughts seem real. We enter lose/lose situations over and over again rather than admit we do not know what we're doing. Often, we'd rather die than admit defeat. That should sound familiar. Why do we continue to engage with those patterns and behaviours that are not working for us? Because we are scared to death. We do not know what awaits us on the other side of "surrender".

Why does not knowing feel scary?

The world has taught you that you must know stuff in order to be important and of value. Everyone wants to be an expert in order to succeed. So, you put on masks and pretend to know some stuff in the hopes that the world will reward you, which it usually does, as long as you play by its rules. That is the catch now. You no longer want to play by its rules.

The reason it feels scary to drop your knowing is that part of you is going to feel unprotected, vulnerable to those things you have come to fear in the world, such as scarcity, failure, and alienation. Ah, but all that awful stuff is exactly what you are rising above. Just as you know there is lack, there is also abundance. You have seen all those opposites plenty of times. Right now, you are making the decision to focus on what you want instead of what you do not want. And surrendering all those old patterns is part of the process.

Whenever a strong emotion arises, it is important to surrender to it and all your thoughts about it, rather than trying to rationalise or logically attempt to sort out your feelings. The fact is, if a feeling is there, it is there. Refrain from blaming or attacking anyone or anything and surrender. It is the most effective way of releasing it and eventually rising above it. As you continue to soften and expand your energetic frequency much of the past will become clearer to you, but from a different perspective. Your past will be one filled with forgiveness. There will be no finger pointing or scapegoating others or yourself. There are no victims. Every person and all the events in your life served to shape you. As you grow in awareness of self-responsibility, you will find this view liberating.

By surrendering all your worries and woes, you make space to amplify your trust, faith, transparency, and gentleness. These are the qualities of true leaders. Drop the fight. Go beyond it. Feel more, and think a whole lot less. When you do think, focus only on thoughts that feel loving and in alignment with unity.

For some of you, you may have already surrendered (more than once). For others, this will be very uncomfortable, bringing up anger and resistance. Breathe through it all and trust that your feel good life is on the other side of everything you thought you knew. Stay present and surrender. Be courageous and drop into your inner vastness. Look around in silent curiosity. See the beauty in you?

We are not here to fix each other. We are here to guide, expand, love, and enjoy. We are telling a new story now, one that reverses the old story of attack and defence. A cosmic story of boundless love long forgotten. Surrender so you can remember that story, and then together we can tell it once more.

5.2 Time

"It takes no time to fall in love, but it takes you years to know what love is." Jason Mraz

When in a loving state, many experience timelessness, which raises the question, "How are we, as a collective, experiencing time? What is it?"

According to Google's top definition, "Time is the indefinite continued progress of existence and events in the past, present, and future regarded as a whole." So, time is indefinite and regarded as a whole. And wholeness is oneness, an unbroken experience of existence. Is this how you experience time? Probably not.

With regards to living in the system, we have chosen to see time as a measure, defined in minutes, hours, and days, etcetera. This measure is useful to us in a lot of ways, because we can stick to schedules, plans, meet deadlines, and so on. If, however, your perception of time is creating stress and a feeling of limitation, then you need to, A) become aware of it and, B) change your perception of it.

Our current use of time is as a limited quantity. People say things like, "I don't have enough time", "There's no time for this". My personal favourite is, "Time is money". Now, refer back to lesson 1.5 Beyond Words, and start to pay attention to how you feel about these "words" which relate time to a thing we are short of, or will run out of.

The thought that you are running out of time is scary. Fortunately, you are super powerful and you needn't perpetuate this version of time any longer. You are going to steal back time in order to enjoy an easy and effortless life.

Begin the deduction process for yourself by asking questions like," "What is the rush?" Or better, "What is time to me?"

****

After my earliest spiritual awakenings, I travelled to England by myself as a backpacker. I spent a lot of my days walking slowly through London, sitting in cafés or on benches, observing people. One day, I remember thinking, "What is the rush? Where is everyone going?" I sensed the pressure and unease of dozens of individuals who seemed stressed out and scared to death, mindlessly rushing around in search of money, or fame, or whatever. What was missing was joy. I felt no sense of connected-ness or even aliveness. It felt to me that humanity was lost, bro-ken, and indeed, it was a reflection of how I felt about myself at that time. From that point forward, I was on a mission to enjoy my life and seek the answers that could liberate not just me, but all these other wonderful human beings, too.

****

Now, it is your turn. Take time to observe life around you. Sit in a café, or on a park bench, and observe people and nature, too. Ask yourself questions and listen inwardly for feel good an-swers. There is no right or wrong, this is just about you redefin-ing your perception of reality so that it feels good to you. You might surprise yourself and in the same moment free yourself from a limiting perception. In so doing, you create more time and eventually, find that you have plenty of time to enjoy your won-derful life.

This is what living in the present moment is all about: dis-solving the illusion of time as a limiting construct and expanding it into an unlimited one. You have the power to do this. Every sin-gle moment is a choice and if you notice yourself getting wrapped up in your busy-ness, and projecting way into the fu-ture, you will likely begin to feel contracted, thinking there's not enough time to get it all done. This is distorted thinking so step back, breathe deeply, and remind yourself, there is infinite time and I always get it done with ease. Resume your activities from this more relaxed and easy place.

Remember, if you want more time, create it for yourself. Assure yourself that you have all the time you need. You hold all the power within you. Keep going, you are amazing.

BONUS LESSON
Money

Like everything else in this Universe, money is a form of energy which carries with it a certain vibrational frequency. It is also man-made and anything man-made can be dissolved and recreated into something different (hint, hint).

We have established that time is not money, unless you are still under the illusion that it is. If the latter is true, you are focussed solely on supporting your external reality and in denial of the internal reality. Through this mass denial, the idea of money is becoming ever more convoluted, and you could say it is polarising us with "the rich get richer, the poor get poorer" kind of thing. As the system continues to propagate a lack of resources for the many, the few remain in ivory towers of denial. But you are not here to fix or change other people. You are here to lift the lid on your own denial and take full responsibility for your inner world, which includes all of your projections, judgments, and limiting beliefs. As you do the inner work, your relationship to money will change, it is inevitable.

Money is a symbol that represents an energetic exchange. Instead of taking responsibility for the creation of it, the large majority of people are still holding beliefs and assumptions about what money is. For example, "money is the root of all evil", or this ridiculous saying, "money makes the world go round". In order to rise above the limitation of a false perception regarding money, you need to take full responsibility for how you feel and think about it, and then change what does not feel good.

Ultimately, money represents your true feelings of worthiness. If you, consciously or unconsciously, feel unworthy, you will deny yourself love and joyful fulfilment. At your core, if you feel worthless, at some point along your journey you absorbed that thought believing it to be true. As a result, you unconsciously push money away, because you feel unworthy of it. Ask yourself what you are unworthy of? It is not actually money, but rather, a feeling of love, purpose, and prosperity. Your core feeling of unworthiness is blocking you from feeling all of it. And we know that any block is a judgment which needs to be dissolved.

Once you align with loving vibrations, the resources you need will naturally show up. You need to be diligent about dissolving harmful assumptions and beliefs about the power money has over you. Remember, nothing has any power over you, unless you let it.

Remind yourself often that you are an infinitely powerful creator of abundance. Continue to transform heavy and divisive judgmental thoughts into lighter ones that reflect your higher-self, the self that is oh so worthy! Follow your heart and surrender what you think you know to be true. Replace any doubt and worry with gratitude. Before you know it, you will be guided into greater service, and your sense of worth will sky rocket. You are SO worth it!

Keep sharing. I love you!

5.3 Arrogance: Ego Grasping

In 3.1, we discussed ego and how it is not a separate thing which manipulates you. You are your ego. It was also previously noted that ego is neither good, nor bad, but an idea. The difficulty that arises initially is getting clear about all of this back and forth and splitting up of ourselves. We do talk about an inner voice, a higher self, or the conscious mind. Are these separate parts of us? No, they are how we have come to define the "whole". So, ego is part of the whole.

The goal of living a fearless life is to move away from labels, especially ones that are misused or that malign, but they can also help us understand deeper concepts. We just need to be conscious of our use of them.

Although there are a few definitions of ego, the simplest defines it as our sense of self-esteem, or self-importance. It serves a purpose and is a good thing, unless it goes astray. Ego run amuck is destructive. It is the part of you that thinks you can fix people because you have all the answers. It is the part of you that judges others. Collectively, the down-side of ego justifies dominion over this planet acting out 'I' opposed to other, instead of, 'I' as one with other.

Throughout the centuries, wisdom teachers talked of our interconnectedness. Their messages convey an ideology of oneness. Many revelled in this thinking, but others feared it knowing individuals who were sovereign over themselves could not be dominated. Those who wanted to keep hold of their power-over retold the stories to suit their desires. That is how beautiful thought becomes distorted.

Lately, with the help of the World Wide Web, myths are being busted. The "average" person can access information once available for a select few, information that reaffirms our oneness. There is no point denying it. We are one. Your ego and you are one. The "you" that judges, resists, and needs to be right at any cost, is the same you that surrenders, allows, and loves unconditionally. It is all up to you.

Choices are offered and no one makes them for you. You can choose the correct response in all things. From this perspective, the ego that would prefer to run the show, begins to dissolve. From a place of strength, the distorted ego melts away leaving you in a more loving vibrational field. Where you once saw competition and corruption, you now see peace and beauty. Where you once felt worthless, or justified in your anger, you now feel loved. This, my friends, is how we are, one loving breath at time, going to transform this world we share.

A distorted ego presents as arrogance. I am challenged by it regularly. As a "spiritual teacher" with insight and a desire to share that insight, I share myself as openly and lovingly as I can, and must still have the courage to admit I know nothing for certain. I have to lovingly allow people to be who they are, and honour their own power, path, and free will. My work then, is to be true to what I teach by holding myself accountable. Perhaps most important of all is to have faith that Love is working through everyone, whether I think it or not.

Continue to be diligent in your practice. Feel your feelings fully and honour each and every one of them. Choose love and unknowing instead of believing you know what's best for others and the world. This may be a great challenge for many of you because you care so deeply, and desire peace on Earth, so badly. I understand, but I often need to remind myself that peace begins within.

Be vulnerable and gentle with yourself. Watch as your distorted ego grasps for survival. Note your arrogance which tells you, you know what you are doing here, and what's best for other people.

Stop fighting thoughts that don't deserve your attention anymore. Continue to heal your own pain so that you can truly be of service to your brothers and sisters who need your help. The innocents who have fallen into darkness, 'lost souls' who have been pushed aside need your light to shine for them. Ignore the world of fear and visualise the world you desire to see in its place. See your paradise. It is your inheritance, your birth right, and there is no time like the present to claim it.

Be aware that change strikes suddenly. Maybe you've spent your whole life chasing a certain amount of money, a specific body size, or an idealised family picture. You are at a point where it is all coming together, when your husband decides to leave, or you get fired. Intense emotional upheaval descends onto your cookie-cutter life. Awful, yes, but there is hope.

If you take responsibility and sit with your pain, when it passes and you rise, you begin again on a higher level. The alternative is believing an ego that wants to blame everyone and make you out to be a victim. The truth is, you are never a failure and there's no one to blame, not even yourself. You can transform, and transforming means breaking down so you can breakthrough - over and over again.

As discussed, this material is not a quick fix, but an ever expanding journey. You are making a radical shift in how you perceive this reality. You are wiping the old hard drive and downloading a whole new program. The conditions will change as you change and your circumstances will morph as you morph. Get excited about your new found power, and about the awesomeness you are going to experience. You've waited a long time for this. You've dreamed about it for ages.

So, drop the arrogance, and focus on you, at least for now. Keep dropping into your own inner space and then expand that inner space out. That is your work, and it's the most important work any of us could be doing now.

Keep going. You are stronger and more beautiful than you know. Believe it. I love you so deeply and one day, you'll feel what I feel. How do I know? Because we are one.

5.4 Free Will

Free will means just that; you can choose. Free will has no morality clause attached to it, hence you can choose up or down, left or right, love or apathy. Free will is a truly divine aspect of our existence here on Planet Earth and you get to choose how you perceive the world, or how you want to experience your existence. Free will secures that right. As you continue to transform old patterns that do not align with your higher-self, it becomes second nature to surrender free will. In other words, you trust your body to tell you what feels right – for you.

One reason you cannot fix other people is because they, too, have free will. Their pain and conditioning might be preventing them from getting in touch with their emotions, but their path is theirs to walk. This work is about feeling the depth of your emotional body and digging up the dense energies weighing you down. Some people feel safer under all that weight. It is better than facing their feelings. As acts of love and gratitude spread, however, more and more people will feel freer to go deep. Momentum, baby! In the meantime, keep working on yourself and trust that everyone is walking their own perfect path. Eventually, they'll find their way to Love.

From the awesome Wayne Dyer, "When you have the choice between being right and being kind just choose kind." That is a great use of free will I'd say.

Free Will Meditation Practice

Use this meditation whenever you are annoyed, angered, or upset by someone else's behaviour, especially someone you feel a powerful connection to, and who you believe to be closed or locked in painful patterns. There is no time limit. Follow your own instincts.

Sitting quietly in your meditation station, light a candle for the person. Focus on the light, bring an image of the person into your conscious awareness, and slowly close your eyes. Breathe deeply and connect to your heart.

As you focus on your breath, begin to fill your body with light and then surround the other person in light as well. Be aware of any feelings that arise within you, and breathe through them, until they are gone. Hold the vision of both of you in the light.

As you sense your worry or upset dissolve, imagine the other person joyful and fulfilled.

Be willing to distance yourself from this person while holding them in the light of your love. Repeat this exercise whenever you need to.

Important: Never forget how truly powerful you are. Choose to imagine that same loving power in everyone, no matter what.

5.5 What To Expect

Expect to feel more flexible, more self-aware, and grounded in your choices. You are deepening your connection to yourself and as you ground your new found, loving awareness deeper into your being, expect to experience greater insights about who you truly are.

Expect people to start looking at you differently and perhaps reacting to you in a way that you may perceive as negative. It is not your negativity, but their own. As you become lighter, your light will illuminate darkness in others, which may make them feel uncomfortable. Remember your work is not to react, but to stay centred and be willing to walk away if needed, while imagining them in the light. On the flip-side, your light will attract more light into your life. Be grateful for that.

Take care of your heart as it opens in this new way. Trust that you will find the people you resonate with and surround yourself with these people; they are your true family and will protect and support you through your darkest hour.

You are surrendering now and this will soften you, delicately removing your hard edges of control. Let it be so. Herein lies your true gifts and talents that you will come to share with the world.

Diligently permission yourself and others to feel good and follow their dreams expecting them to come true. Because they will.

You are a shining star. Shine bright!

BONUS LESSON
Deep Breathing

Deep breathing is exactly what it sounds like. In our modern day, stressed-out busy-ness, no one is breathing deeply enough and, as a result, are stifling their first access point to depth of feeling and expanded awareness.

There are many benefits to breathing deeply, including toning the abdominal floor, massaging the internal organs, expanding lung capacity, and calming the mind, to name a few. Breathing deeply requires focus, which is always good for the mind.

Breathing is directly linked to the nature of your thoughts, so if you want to have access to deeper, more inspired thought, you need to start breathing more deeply. You can breathe deeply anytime, anywhere, just be comfortable and relaxed. If you are not relaxed, breathing deeply will help.

Focus on breathing in as slowly and steadily as you can, from the root upward. This means, imagining that you are inhaling from your feet upwards, filling up your seat, lower abdomen, and your tummy, before moving to your rib cage and back, sternum, chest, collar bones and throat, and finally reaching the crown of your head. Gently suspend the breath at the top of your inhale for just a beat, then exhale all the way down, from your head to your feet, slowly and steadily.

On the exhale, make sure you are releasing completely. Feel your lungs and all your tummy muscles contract as you near the end of your exhalation. Similarly, when you have exhaled completely, pause for a beat before you begin the next inhalation.

Practice this as frequently as possible and continue to expand your breath awareness. Have fun with it! How deep can you breathe? How slow can you go? Make it a fascinating game of inner exploration and enjoy!

Step 5. Surrender Knowing

Exercise A.

Write down what surrender means to you. Be prepared to share.

Exercise B.

Can you choose one thing you think you know and describe what it means to you? Keep it small, for example, a pillow or an apple. Be prepared to share.

Exercise C.

At this point, is there anything you are asking yourself to surrender? Write it down and be willing to share.

Exercise D.

Take time to observe life around you. Sit in a café, or on a park bench. Observe people or nature. Ask yourself questions and listen inwardly for feel good answers. There is no right or wrong. This exercise is about you redefining your perception of reality so that it feels good to you. You might surprise yourself and in the same moment liberate yourself from a limiting perception. In so doing, you create more time and eventually, live in total ease and timelessness…all the time.

It is strongly recommended to not write down notes during this exercise as it is an observational practice in awareness and presence. Write down a few notes after you have completed this exercise and be prepared to discuss.

Exercise E.

Begin to imagine your perfect world. What does it look like? Write it down and even put some pictures in there. Build momentum within your own energy by making it specific and really buying into its reality. Feel it. Put it on your vision board and be willing to make changes to it whenever you feel necessary. It is your world.

Exercise F.

Use this meditation whenever you are annoyed, angered or upset by someone else's behaviour, especially someone you feel a powerful connection to and you perceive that they are closed or in deeply painful patterns.

Sitting quietly in your meditation station, light a candle for the person in mind. Focus on the candle, bring an image of the person into your awareness and slowly close your eyes. Breathe deeply and connect to your heart space.

As you focus on your breath begin to fill your body with light. And then, in your mind surround the other person in light as well. Be aware of any feelings that arise within you and breathe through them, ushering their transformation. Maintain your light.

As you sense your worry or upset dissolve, imagine the other person in their joy and aligned with Divine Will, whatever that looks like to you. Sit with this practice until you feel free. Repeat this exercise whenever needed and with whoever triggers an emotional response in you that you feel is 'their' pain.

Be willing to distance yourself from this person and continue to hold them in the light of your loving awareness while imagining the highest vision for yourself and the other.

Important: Never forget how truly powerful you are. Choose to imagine that same loving power in everyone, no matter what.

Step 6. Meditation, Mindfulness & Routine

6.1 What is Meditation?

Meditation is simply paying attention to the energy that is you. It is an act of withdrawing, or disengaging your focus on the external world, which includes thought, and becoming aware of your awareness, or consciousness - that part of you that is a witness to your thoughts, feelings, and everything else.

Meditation is not, as many modern and somewhat distorted teachings would have you think, about escaping your body or emptying your mind. This may happen occasionally when you drop deeply enough into your awareness, but escaping your body, or emptying your mind is not the goal; there is no goal. How can there be no goal? Because, you are already it. In the words of the renowned spiritual teacher, Ram Dass, "All that you seek is already within you."

People often work toward material goals. When they achieve what they've been seeking they feel a sense of satisfaction. Unfortunately, all too often, that satisfaction is short lived. People find they are no happier or peaceful once they get what they were after, so off they go, continuing the search for what is missing in their lives.

The same is true in the internal world of self-awareness. People seek enlightenment through spiritual teachers, and despite having followed all the "rules", cannot find the light. Why is that? Because they are still seeking external, quick-fix style, solutions. They are avoiding the real inner work by taking on all kinds of external tasks, but missing the point completely. They must be the change they seek.

Meditation is a technique to rest the mind and attain a state of consciousness that is totally different from the normal waking state. It is the means for reaching into, in order to better understand, all the levels of ourselves, and finally experiencing the centre of consciousness within.

Because what you see around you is a mirror-like reflection of your very own vibrational frequency, if you want to see something different you must change your perception of things. A meditative state can keep you closer to your higher-self and keep you focussed on change that aligns with your true purpose here. You can continue to imagine your preferences, and feel your way to better feelings guided by a growing awareness from within. Gradually, you begin to embody the change, raising your frequency and vibrating that which you have desired.

In simple terms, if you want to see more love in the world, you must become more loving. If you want to see more fairness in the world, practice fairness. If you want to see more abundance in the world, practice giving. The only real challenge any of us face is finding the courage to love our darkness.

Regular practice benefits body and mind by helping the practitioner accept themselves completely, foibles and all. The practice expands your conscious awareness and illuminates your darkness. Of course, you can run away, but running away from your darkness will only perpetuate limiting and potentially destructive behaviours.

Once seen, dense emotions start to lose some of their power over you. Hopefully, you have already realised a degree of this through your emotional triggers, waves, and storms experience. Tapping into your consciousness through meditation, helps you see that the darkest and densest stuff is your greatest teacher. The darkness is begging to be acknowledged and transformed, not abhorred. Heavy old emotional wounds are begging to be healed, not buried. Realising this makes forgiving easy because you now understand that you are here to feel it all and rise above. You are here to learn to love it all. How can we evolve completely unless we learn what it means to be truly alive human beings? We cannot.

If you are ready, commit to your inner exploration and raise your awareness so you can finally experience the life you seek. Commit to your dreams, sit down, shut up, and get to know who you truly are. Your meditation station awaits, and is your best chance of figuring yourself out.

6.2 Silence: Steal Back Time

In a loud world, silence is the most powerful antidote. It is within your own silent awareness that you can access your timeless nature and then reclaim eternal timelessness. Silence is the void. Get to know it and you are well on your way to a lasting peace. Coming into silence is another way to honour your totality without judgment. It is a paradox, which is why it does not make sense to everyone. You are everything and nothing. You are the sound and the silence. You are the darkness and the light. When you know nothingness, you can fully experience "everything". When you get to know your silence, you can choose the sound you desire. Get to know your darkness so that you can bask in your own light.

How do you get silent? Meditation. How do you get to know nothingness? Stop believing your thoughts are true. How do you get to know your darkness? Feel your dense emotions. BOOM. You are done. Ha-ha! Really, you are, you probably just do not believe it yet. You will soon.

Own the fact that you are part of everything you see around you, otherwise you would not see it. Own the fact that you have desired your creation, otherwise, you would not exist. Own the fact that in silence you expand your awareness.

In silence, there is no trying. You do not need to try to be silent. Silence is the ever-present background of all noise, you need only tune into it, rather than the noise. If you are hearing birds chirping and they are starting to piss you off, be aware that there is a part of you choosing to be pissed off. The birds are neutral and are not trying to upset you. Own your awareness and feel your feelings. Don't blame the birds! Ha! Wild stuff. Out of this world, truly.

Now, because silence aligns with timelessness, in the silence there is no timeline, so actually, there's no rush. Rushing around is stressful. Relax, you have infinite time. Yes, you really do. Paradoxically, the more you relax, the faster and easier your transformation will be. The reward is that you get to truly enjoy your life and all the people in it.

Enlightenment does not look like anything. A person can practice yoga, master the postures, look good in tights and sit for hours in meditation, but they still hold judgment by claiming someone else is "un-yogic" if they do not practice every day, or if they drink alcohol. Judgment is not yoga. Yoga is a 'yoking' practice, an eight-fold path designed to merge the small self with the broader self, the separate will with oneness. This is more about perspective than fancy postures.

Do not misunderstand me, yoga is awesome and powerful, but ultimately, you need to find what makes sense for you. Only you can do this. As long as you are seeking yourself in someone else's version of yoga, you will likely not find what you are looking for because there is no one right way for everyone, there is only your way.

Going into the silence helps you find your way. It is your greatest ally. Get to know it.

6.3 Mindfulness: Meditation in Action

I often hear people say, "Oh yes, I practice mindfulness, but I can't meditate." Huh? Here we go again, more excuses, diversions, and deflections to actually taking responsibility. Mindfulness is meditation. It is a way of life. It is meditation in action.

Living mindfully means you are taking responsibility for your actions, and thoughts. When mindful, you are not blaming or attacking the external world. Your daily meditation practice is what grounds you in your ability to be mindful consistently. Otherwise, you are just too easily distracted by the distorted mind and your deeply ingrained reactive patterns. So, when someone says they practice mindfulness but not meditation, they are sort of missing the point. Well meaning, I am sure, but certainly in denial of what the real work entails.

Mindfulness is the art of paying attention, just like meditation. In meditation, you are alone, usually in a quiet room, undistracted. Mindfulness is a meditative practice done while you are doing stuff, and relating to other people. This is when remaining in a meditative state becomes a real challenge.

Let's be honest, we can all remain chilled out and peaceful when no one else gets involved. But that ain't life! We are all involved with each other, whether we like it or not. We share a planet for crying out loud!

Sitting with, and having the courage to dissolve your emotional densities is the point of mindfulness, but, like yoga and lots of other powerful practices, these techniques have been distorted by human minds unwilling to look deeper and take full responsibility, mainly because they are still too afraid to face their own pain. "People have a hard time letting go of their suffering. Out of a fear of the unknown, they prefer suffering that is familiar." Thich Nhat Hanh. And, you know this already; it is all okay. Love everyone, no matter what they choose. Just be willing to walk away from the people who choose to suffer. Their suffering will only cause you more pain. You, on the other hand, are ready to take responsibility, face the unknown, and feel the fullness of your vibrational mess so you can clean it up.

Mindfulness is a radically effective tool for transformation. Humanity's structured and systematised thinking gets us lost in defining, categorising, and over-analysing. It ends up the ultimate peace-zapper because of an obsession with being right. Let's say there is no right or wrong. We are all just trying to figure it out; this thing we call Life.

You are more powerful than you realise and more capable than you give yourself credit for. Start believing in your power. Meditate more, become mindful in every area of your life and presto! A new and better life unfolds.

Make the practice your own. Call it whatever you want. Mindfulness is just you paying attention to your breathe while speaking, or your feet when walking. You could liken it to awareness embodied. And it is really cool.

Mindfulness tip: Whenever you feel an uncomfortable emotion, locate it, label it and accept it. For example: Someone cuts you off in traffic and you feel angry. First, locate it. Notice where it is in your body. Then, label it with something like, "Oh, hello anger." Then accept it by assuring yourself it is okay to feel anger. Finally, breathe through it, practice your deep breathing and do not attack or judge the other driver for cutting you off. Continue to breathe deeply until the emotion dissolves. Job done. You have successfully transformed some dense energy. Hurray!

BONUS LESSON
Conscious Eating

Just like your meditation practices, there are ways you can invoke more mindfulness into your life by setting time aside to practice. I have chosen conscious eating because there's a lot of collective issues around food and consumption in general. I'm not here to tell you what to eat, except to choose food that truly makes you feel good. If there are food issues in your life, however, conscious eating can help you work through them and begin to love food and life again.

The best way to establish a new pattern is to try it out by yourself for a bit. Eventually, it will become the norm, whether you are eating with your family, on a date, or with a big group of people. So, create some time for yourself when you can practice eating consciously.

Here's what you are going to do. Grab some food. Before putting it in your mouth, look at it. Really look at it. Imagine it is something you have never seen before; observe it with an innocent curiosity. Then go further. Smell it, touch it, and make sweet love to it. Ha! I am kidding, but not really.

In order to dissolve your food issues, you need to stop judging food. Food, like anything else outside of you, is not the enemy. As you relinquish your judgment toward food, you will be better able to honour your body's desire to nourish itself. Once you feel you have sufficiently observed, and lovingly related to your food choice, take a bite and continue to pay attention like you have never paid attention before. Feel the texture as it enters your mouth, feel your taste-buds firing, notice all the sensations as you chew and then, swallow. Feel it as it moves through your throat, oesophagus, and then enters your stomach. Notice it all. How is it making you feel? Be grateful for it. You have just been nourished!

Do this every day until you notice yourself eating more mindfully even in public situations. Honour your desires. If you want cake, eat some cake. If you want a salad, have a salad. Be grateful for the abundance of food you have available to you; it is a privilege afforded to too few. Share what you are doing with loved ones. Notice how your food choices change. This practice will not only change your relationship to food, but your body as well. I am sure you have heard the saying, "you are what you eat"? Well, I'd like to change it to "you are how you eat!" Slow down. Be mindful. Be thankful. You are awesome. And so is food.

6.4 Routine: Personal Love Rituals

When establishing your new life, creating special daily routines or, you could call them your personal love rituals, is really important. They help you stay focussed and continue to ground you into your new reality. Think of it this way, everything

147

you do is a locked-down pattern. As you make the shift, you want to make darn sure you are locking down those new, more elevated, patterns.

Creating new patterns is a continual, creative process that really does require a commitment in the form of ritualised routines. You know this because you have already started by creating a meditation station, and using it daily. You can also see the patterns you support at a lower frequency, those denser energetic patterns that are less than desirable 'ritualised' behaviours like a crappy job, excessive partying, binge eating, fighting with people, and so on.

Routine does not mean rigidity. Sacred ritual is about performing more loving and enlightening activities regularly. It does not mean becoming a drill sergeant who beats you up if you miss a day. It does not even mean you have to do the exact same thing every day, either. Rigidity comes from control, from a sense of lack, or not being good enough, so you feel that you need to rigidly control your external reality in order to be safe. This is not the aim of this lesson. Your love rituals should be much softer and more fluid.

You have already established a daily gratitude meditation, divine spark meditation, and your conscious eating practice. Great start! Now, I encourage you to go further. Your new love rituals are about empowering and strengthening your connection to your new life in a profound and loving way, consistently.

Should you decide against establishing new sacred rituals on a daily basis, you risk slipping into that old default setting much more easily. Your presence awareness is your bedrock, and if you are not grounding yourself in it throughout the day, every day, and lovingly reinforcing the new you, old patterns re-surface. Stay strong. Stay committed.

Love rituals can consist of many things. Choose ones that feel good to you alongside your daily meditations and conscious eating. Move. Breathe. Dance. Practice activities that fill you with joy, intend they be sacred celebrations, because that is what you are doing, celebrating your star power.

For some of you, at least in the beginning, you may need to plan it out with a list, for example. It might look like this in your diary:

5am: Meditation. 5:20am: Move around playfully. 5:30am: Eat some grub consciously. 6am: Brush my teeth and smile at myself in the mirror, admiring my own radiant beauty.

Get the picture? You can totally re-programme your life, switch it all up in the most loving way possible. At some point, if some of the stuff you started out with begins to feels stagnant or less than enjoyable, switch it up again. For example:

10am: Wake-up, stretch and be super-duper thankful for my awesome life. 10:15am: Sit down quietly, breathe deeply, and imagine how wonderful my day is going to be. 10:30am: Eat some delicious food, give massive hugs to my whole family, and tell them how much I love them. 11am: Go for a run and admire the beauty of the outdoors.

Seriously, I cannot emphasise this enough. Do stuff that makes you feel good, not what you think is right or good. You have to feel this one out, big time. The degree of your love and joy is the most important thing, not pleasing other people, or fitting into a box society tells you, you are supposed to fit into. Nope. You are breaking free from all that, and beginning to play with life again.

So, go play. Cut out the stuff that brings you down and replace it with what lifts you up, even if it feels weird. Even if you think you are lying to yourself. You will only feel this way because your default setting is fighting back, telling you that you are not worth it, and that none of this stuff will really work. I am here to tell you, this stuff does work as long as you believe it will.

If your new awesomeness triggers people around you, send them love and let them in on your secret if you are called to do so. Your new patterns will have the right people showing up for you, new friends who dig your unique weirdness. People who are inspired by your epic LOVE vibrations will appear. Trust it, they will find you. Why? You are shining your light and they can finally see the real you!

Thing is, the system prides itself on uniformity. It likes "grey" and encourages masks of denial. It promotes the "us against them" mentality. You can breakthrough by bringing your imagination to life. Do what you love, and love what you do, every day. Act as if you have always been that free, that shiny, that loud, that joyful, and that effervescent. This is your tipping point. Once you start to establish your new physical patterns you are off! NO excuses.

Stay easy. Stay soft. Do not worry if you dip back into your default setting, just notice it, and calmly remind yourself where you are headed. Have faith in the process and most importantly, have faith in YOU. You are it.

Keep up the great work.

6.5 What To Expect

At this stage, you should definitely feel more connected to yourself. You should have a deeper awareness of your oneness in this awesome life you are living. It may not feel consistent, but as you continue your work, and keep to your rituals, you will experience more lightness, serenity and ease.

You should expect more energy and naturally shift to foods and lifestyle choices that make you feel good about yourself.

By now you should have transformed some of the dense guilt, shame, and unworthy vibes. As a result of this transformation, you will begin to notice, in a more obvious way, the effects of these core emotional densities throughout the collective. Jealousy, competition, gossip, comparison, complaining and doubt, to name a few. These are very common in the system and pretty much promoted as the way to be. So, these are often well established in our default setting emotional patterns and they are divisive and destructive. They will more than likely be experienced in waves, rather than emotional storms and you will likely only notice them after the fact, at least at first.

Here's an example. You get intertwined in some gossip and leave the situation feeling bad. Aha! You have spotted low level interaction. Forgive yourself and all involved, then move on with greater awareness. You might want to avoid certain people in the future, or until you feel strong enough to stay centred and not be pulled into gossip. With that written, your path is unique. The most important thing for you to do is to choose to dissolve emotions that do not feel good to you, and always find your way to a loving perspective; one where everybody wins. It is possible.

You should notice that things that once triggered you, no longer do. Big yourself up for that.

You might notice yourself being more generous with your time and money. Hurray, you are changing the world one generous act at a time.

You are rising at light speed, it just might not look like it yet. You are well on your way.

BONUS LESSON
Victorious Breath

Like all the other breath exercises in this book, victorious breath is an incredibly powerful practice and one that comes from good ol' yoga. You will often hear it as, Ujjayi (pronounced oo-jai), which is Sanskrit, yoga's mother tongue. Some refer to it as the "oceanic breath," which is a descriptive expression because it sounds like steady waves gently stroking the shore.

The benefits of victorious breath are many, so you will want to do it a lot. To name a few, victorious breath increases oxygen in the blood, relieves tension, calms the mind, soothes the nervous system, regulates blood pressure, promotes energy flow, and increases your presence awareness. This is a superb breath practice for conscious movement and meditation. To top it off, it helps dissolve irritation and frustration. Yippee!

How to do it? Close your mouth and start to breathe in and out through your nose. Begin to breathe a little deeper and more steadily than you might normally. On your next inhale, very gently constrict (tense) the back of your throat so that you can hear 'the waves crashing' sound as the air passes through the area of your throat. Do the same on the exhale and establish a rhythmic, soothing breathing pattern.

Important note: The constriction should not restrict the air flow or feel tense at all. Play around until you feel a calming, focussing effect.

Step 6. Meditation, Mindfulness & Routine

Exercise A.

If you are not already meditating daily, you must begin now if you want to progress to these higher levels.

Exercise B.

Can you locate one area of your life that is too noisy? Write notes and be prepared to share.

Exercise C.

Try this. Whenever you feel an uncomfortable emotion, locate it, label it and accept it. For example, someone cuts you off in traffic and you feel angry. First, you 'locate it', which means you notice where it is your body. Then, 'label it'. Be like, "Oh, hello anger!" Then 'accept it' with an, "It's okay that I am angry." Finally, breathe through it, practice your deep breathing and do not attack or judge the other driver for cutting you off. Continue to breathe deeply until the emotion shifts. Job done. You have successfully transformed some dense energy. Hurray!

Exercise D.

What would your ideal day look like, write it down and do it. For example, if you have to get up and prepare for a teaching session like me! Then it might look something like this: 5:00am, meditate. 5:20am, move around playfully. 5:30am eat some grub, consciously. 6:00am, brush teeth and smile at self in the mirror, admiring my own radiant beauty.

Get the picture? You can do this. Totally reprogram your day and keep it that way! Then switch it all up in the most loving and awesome way possible. At some point, if the stuff you started out with begins to feel stagnant or less than enjoyable, switch it up again.

Step 7. Living in the Flow

7.1 Patience

"Patience. Learn, you must!" Yoda

Let's all learn from Star Wars' legendary Jedi master, Yoda, and use the force within us to overcome our own darkness! Darth Vader symbolises the illusory dark forces of the mind. Fictional, for real. To overcome the fear and darkness so you can step into living fearlessly, you must summon the force. You do this by becoming fiercely and unconditionally loving towards yourself and everything else in your world.

We all have the power to become Jedi masters. All we need to do is work with our higher-selves to tap into the infinite and unique creative energy within; that is the force. You do not need a light sabre to be a Jedi (unless you really want one). Mental clarity and hard core self-belief, you need! I digress.

In several lessons, I asked you to be patient. I also referred to words and knowing. At this point, rather than just tell you to be patient, I am going to deconstruct the word so that you have a way of accessing the vibrational essence of it.

I am certain many of you have heard the phrase, "patience is a virtue". Now, why is that? And, if that is true, what does it mean to be virtuous? Virtuousness is about integrity, dignity, and worthiness. It is all the goodness in us. Patience is about you upholding the goodness of yourself and others in any situation.

There are three main definitions of the word patience:

1. The quality of being patient, as the bearing of provocation, annoyance, misfortune, or pain, without complaint, loss of temper, irritation, or the like.

2. An ability or willingness to suppress restlessness or annoyance when confronted with delay.

3. A quiet, steady perseverance; even-tempered care; diligence.

Let's look at that first definition, of ...bearing... pain without...loss of temper. Now, to me, this wreaks of denial. Why? Because if you are irritated, you are irritated. Telling yourself to be patient will only mask the irritation. So, let's scrap that first definition.

Onto number two, an ability... to suppress... annoyance when confronted with delay. Again, you are not here to suppress anything. That is resistance and we know what that does! Furthermore, you cannot pretend to be patient when you are actually annoyed. You need to recognise that you are annoyed and then deal with it. So, we'll scrap that definition, too.

Finally, definition number three, a quiet, steady perseverance. Now we're onto something.

Like Yoda's wise words, "patience, learn you must", you must be patient with yourself as you learn a new way of being.

This new way of being means fully feeling all that you are, accepting yourself and taking responsibility for it. Not masking, not suppressing, and not blaming.

Patience is an antidote to the impatience driven by the quick fix mentality of popular culture. We all want results yesterday and when we do not get them, we blame the product, the government, our family, or ourselves for not being enough. We attack ourselves for not having enough money, for not wearing the right clothes, or for not being the right size. This latter mentality especially is killing us, literally. Many have become like the walking dead or the storm troopers of the dark forces.

Patience is not something you do, it is a state of being achieved by getting to know yourself fully. Within yourself, you establish that quiet, steady perseverance by staying connected to your intuition and having faith that your loving dreams can, and will, come true.

You are not here to suppress, deny, or even try to uphold the moral standards that the world teaches. You are here to experience your unique life and to be of service. Much of the world is corrupt, you do not need to always be nice. Sometimes you need to get angry, feel it and own it because you are angry for a reason. Until you own that anger, the world will continue to corrupt you.

Patience is a natural way of being when you are in a loving state with yourself and all of life. There is no rush, because there is no goal; there is nowhere else you are meant to be. You are here already.

Have faith in your abilities. Your patience supports your diligence and commitment to loving transformation. Through patience you have the ability to love ALL, no matter what. You can draw on your experiences and bestow patience because you have been there.

If you feel impatient, breathe. Your ego is grasping for its arrogant survival and telling you it knows what is best. It does not, otherwise you'd be completely at peace already.

It is all going to be okay. We are all wounded to a certain degree and as we rise, collectively, we are facing and healing those wounds. Being fearless enough to stand down your judgments, fears, and worries means you are making space for more loving energy to take their place.

So, be patient. You are being guided all the time, and when you feel impatient, know that in that moment, you are resisting your higher self's guidance. Fall back. Listen. Trust. Patience really is a virtue and it truly is, "… the key which solves all problems." Sudanese Proverb

7.2 Detachment

There is a lot of talk about detachment especially in "spiritual" circles. It took me a long time to really get a sense of what the word means, practically speaking.

In simple terms, detachment means you remain neutral, impartial, and objective. It does not mean that you do not care, or that you are unaware. It is quite the opposite. With regards to this material, detachment means that you are so gosh-darn grounded that nothing outside of you can provoke a reaction; you are not swayed, rather, you remain an observer, radiating loving frequencies everywhere you go.

An often challenging concept regarding detachment is separating your masks, or persona, from the real you. In other words, you are not essentially your name, your thoughts, your body or your job, these are the masks created by you and the collective. You are not your ideas, opinions, or your shenanigans. What you are is energy in motion and vast undisturbed stillness. The other stuff is what has been established to define identities. They are labels, impermanent creations made by you to help you expand and get to know more of who you truly are.

When feeling peaceful, neutral, spacious, innocent, and playful, you are as you are meant to be. When you are not feeling that way, the goal is to find your way back to good feelings. But how?

You have a choice to detach completely from thoughts that do not feel good to you. Repeat: You have a choice to detach completely from thoughts that do not feel good to you. It does not matter how real or important you think something is. Ultimately, if it feels contracted, if it hurts you, listen up. You are being told that something you are doing, or thinking, is not working for your highest good.

Even so-called spiritual communities get all distorted by this. People seek transcendence through denial. They give up alcohol or chocolate, stretch their bodies into impossible postures, and meditate for hours. They speak in hushed tones, wear robes and burn incense. It does not matter what you do or don't do, how spiritual you think you are, if you are resisting something within you, or judging others for being less than you or wrong, you are not getting to the heart of energetic transformation.

It is easy today to become apathetic and complacent in what seems like a world gone mad. A lot of us want change, but we have not got a clue how to make it happen and all too soon, our confusion wears us out. In our exhaustion, alone and feeling defeated, we say to ourselves, "Maybe it is easier to just give in? Give up. Stay silent. Stay small. Who am I to think I can rise above the system?" This is powerless thinking - not detachment.

Detachment, for this guide, means that you are prepared to let go of worry, doubt, and fear. Once gone, you have made space for more of what feels good. So, take a breath, step away from the troubles you are seeing, and harmonise your vibes until the world of fear no longer triggers you. That is transformation. That is detachment. You will know you have succeeded because you will feel more consistently peaceful and calm.

You are always creating a spectrum of emotions which you experience directly through your feeling body. Feelings of stress, worry, panic, jealousy, or anger add to a spectrum which is on a much lower frequency than love. If you are living in one, or any combination, of those former states, you will find yourself on edge and stressed out. Not the best place to be, obviously. Taking responsibility for yourself and claiming your power to not think certain thoughts, ushers you into a more loving state. You are learning to detach. Remind yourself that just because you are habitually thinking certain thoughts does not make them real. Just because there appears to be lots of scary stuff happening out there, does not make it real.

Does some of that sound cuckoo? Well, it kind of is, brilliantly so! And, you have a choice between fearful, impoverished, cuckoo, or love, live-in-paradise, cuckoo. The choice is yours.

This work is not easy. Taking responsibility for all that you are is a massive undertaking. You have decided to face and alter some lifelong energetic themes imprinted in your cellular body! Thinking about it is a time wasting distraction. You have to be able to feel what is going on in your body, and stop buying into the reality of your thoughts. When you are able to truly detach from thought, you become the watcher, witnessing even the most difficult situations, fully present, but with no assumptions or judgments. You are detached yet aware, and vibrating only compassion.

In this state of being, you become a powerful conduit for peace and healing. Your vibrational frequency actually allows, or holds space for, the other to simply "be", whether they are being confrontational, aggressive, or kind, and relaxed, it matters not. When detached, you are peaceful, harmonious, and fully aware. Conversely, when attached, you identify with, and stay bound to, external conditions. You have handed away your power. Detach, bring your power home. Put it back into your loving heart and feel yourself soar.

You are free to "be". You are star power.

7.3 Letting Go

"Train yourself to let go of everything you fear to lose." Yoda

"Just let it go!" You hear it all the time, and is it easy? Ha-ha! Like detachment, I am going to redefine the common understanding of "letting go." It has become synonymous with ignoring, or walking away from, anything that is considered difficult. Instead, I view letting go not as something you do, but, as a state of being. It is like your flow state, deeply aligned with your purpose. What you let go of, over time, is the need to resist or fight against the external world. You no longer seek external gratification or reward, because you know that you are the reward.

You can't change the external world by fighting against it. That creates more fighting. You have to fundamentally change your inner world, and from this inner shift, your external world will naturally transform. Letting go of your need to change all that stuff "out there" frees up a lot of time to focus on feeling good about you.

****

After my early awakenings, I was travelling around Europe and stream writing a lot. During one long train journey, as I gazed at the passing scenery, my hand was writing, 'let go, let go, let go, let go' over and over again. I remember feeling peaceful as I wrote, but when I tried to think about it, I could not make

163

sense of its meaning. What was I letting go of? Well, what I have come to realise is that I was letting go of everything. Everything I thought I was, everything I thought I wanted, and indeed, everything I feared losing. (Seriously, if you think you need a master, choose Yoda.)

****

By following the suggestions outlined in the guidebook, you are cultivating this state of being naturally, because you are transforming the emotional densities that keep you bound to fearful drama. Through this process, you enlighten and come to know you have nothing to lose, so external conditions cannot hold onto you unless you choose to let them. No matter how mean someone is to you, or how crazy the world appears to be getting, you are not triggered. You have dissolved, or transformed the emotions that caused the reaction and so you are not carrying those energy frequencies anymore. That is letting go, like detachment, it is the opposite of holding on or remaining attached to the external conditions.

Step 7 is all about dropping in and letting go, and so acts to usher in higher and higher realms of experience through a childlike return of innocent curiosity, awe, and creativity. When in this state, your new world will begin to dawn.

Remember: You can't just tell yourself to let go, you have to *feel* it. That is what embodiment means. You will know you are letting go when you are no longer being triggered by the same things. Be aware that your triggers will change and become more subtle, but have no fear. You are also developing greater awareness and becoming more skilful at recognising what is going on, so even those super intense storms will not floor you in the same way anymore. You have gained greater clarity with regards to the energy you are being asked to transform. You will be able to manage it or ride it out with more grace, regardless of how intense it feels. This also means that your transformation process is accelerating. Wahoo!

At this point, be very aware of what brings you joy and excitement. Relish those experiences. Let those feelings sink deep into you. Give yourself a massive high-five for the work you are doing. You deserve it. When you are reaching states of bliss and ecstasy, it means your cellular body is holding more of the light frequencies, so let yourself overflow with gratitude.

This is a global movement and your part in it is more important than you could ever know.

"Love you, I do." Yoda.

7.4 Flow State

"Love is a wave flowing in the direction of bliss for all living things. It will carry you if you allow it to flow through you." Marianne Williamson

Living in the flow is a timeless, fluidly loving, state of being. It is joyful, serene, tranquil, and highly creative. The system is the opposite; insidious, rigidly controlling, invasively loud, limited and limiting. Blind uniformity is what holds the system together. Living in the flow dissolves this uniformity through inspired, authentic, creative expression, which comes from the true you.

Children live naturally in a flow state. Each child's life is different, of course, so what they absorb when little, and how they alter their flow is unique. You will notice children do not tend to limit themselves. They express how they feel honestly, in the form of screaming, crying, throwing tantrums, as well as snuggling, playing, and questioning.

When a child is loved unconditionally, and allowed to express themselves honestly, without judgment, they tend to grow into loving, fulfilled adults. But, since the large majority of the human collective is in a vibrational mess, most of us miss out, as did our parents and ancestors. So, no one is to blame for your mess, you have just given yourself the divine task of ground-control-vibrational-cleaning-crew. Taking responsibility is your gateway to freedom. You are a grown up now, after all.

For example, you might think flow is something only professional athletes experience, or super rich people. Not so. In fact, this is another distorted view that has you believing there are 'special' people to worship and idolise, while you remain a lowly and underserving peasant. Do not get me wrong, athletes, and celebrities are awesome, but so are you. You do not need to be 'special' in the eyes of the world in order to enjoy your life. You just need to believe you are worthy of enjoying your life.

Also, as you continue to permission yourself to love and enjoy your unique and glorious aliveness, you will get better acquainted with living in the flow.

Like most of the lessons in this book, flow is not about what you do, but how you do it. We have established that seeking outside yourself for happiness does not work. You do not get happiness from outside things, rather, you feel happiness. And just like all emotions, it is harnessed from within you. Through the harnessing of these different emotional frequencies, your experiences are created, not the other way around. You have surely heard it before, that the car, the house, or the shoes will not make you happy.

There is no judgment around things, however. If you genuinely like driving cool cars, you are totally allowed to, as long as it feels good to you. Your material world can be whatever you desire. If there are aspects of your material world that cause you guilt, however, you need to own and transform that guilt so you can realign with your true purpose and not just go after what you think you are meant to go after. Not everyone wants the fancy house, many are just blinded by the illusion that it will bring them joy. Get over it. Go within and get to know what you truly desire.

Flow living is a recognition that you are everything. Once you are living authentically, doing what resonates with you, flow becomes your natural state of being. You are no longer fighting against conditions. You are merging with them and dissolving the ones that do not serve you. Eventually, transforming becomes second nature. You stop blaming and attacking, and your vibration becomes more water-like. That is flow. You could even become like steam. Jedi Master, you will become. Gotta love the wisdom of Yoda.

Start noticing when you are in a state of timelessness. This state is guiding you. Pay attention to what you are doing, the people you are around, and the places you find yourself when you feel joyous and in love with life. Then, give yourself permission to do more of it. No matter how counterintuitive this might feel in comparison to your default setting, being joyful is your real job. Full stop.

Remind yourself that you are always connected, even when you are feeling low, limited, or less than. It is only your old distorted mind playing tricks on you, making you believe that those feelings are all you deserve. It does not have to be this way. You are an infinite being, having a finite experience. Or, as Pierre Teilhard de Chardin expressed, "We are not human beings having a spiritual experience; we are spiritual beings having a human experience." The good news is that collectively, we are waking up to this concept. More and more, people are tapping into their spiritual essence and living in an infinitely flowing state of grace.

Let go of the old paradigm that tells you the only way to get ahead is through struggle and hard work, through competition and powerlessness. You do not have to believe it. You can get to know your emotional body and use it to climb into ever higher vibrational states. Your day, your job, and your entire life can then be your flow state. It is your birth right, and your choice. You can stay in the low vibes if you want to, but, I do not think you want that.

So, stop making excuses and allow yourself to flow. It feels so good!

BONUS LESSON
Frequency Jumps

This bonus lesson is to let you know that some of your experiences might start to get a bit weird. Shifting into a vibrational awareness, and consciously uplifting yourself, means that once 'normal' situations will begin to feel different to you. It is okay. Do not be afraid.

As you awaken to a broader reality, your senses will change. How you see things will change, too. Stay relaxed and let your intuition guide you. It is showing you your own gifts and talents. Initially, the sight of these might freak you out because your default setting has been denying them for so long. You have successfully kept the doors on your own miraculous nature closed. As you expand and rise you are going to open those doors.

Changes are apparent. Onlookers can't quite figure out what is different about you, so be mindful. Your awareness and intuition will let you know what is going on vibrationally speaking, regardless of how people look at you. This is often called empathy.

Empathy allows you to feel energies around you. As you open your heart and shed layers of masks, your ability to feel the energies of others might grow, too. Stay centred, and remain grounded. Remind yourself to stay detached enough to watch and not react to feelings. It can be very challenging and easy to react to what we believe we are feeling from others. If you are in a crowd, or out with friends, and it all becomes too much, excuse yourself and leave. It does not matter what other people think of you, it matters only that you take responsibility for how you feel, and honour your intuitive guidance.

Please do share your experiences, but remain patient and non-judgmental to others, always. Your awakening, your journey, is ultimately yours alone. Not everyone will understand, or agree with you, and that is okay. Each of us has our own walk to walk.

7.5 Resistance

Resistance opposes the states of detachment, letting go, and flow. It is contraction, struggle, and supports judgments, assumptions, and limiting beliefs.

Carl Jung said, "What you resist, persists". In other words, if you push against a belief, thought stream, or emotion, you perpetuate it. We tend to resist many things almost instinctively, but in order to coexist within and without, it is time to let go, detach, and allow that which we have resisted for generations.

Resistance manifests itself as tension, stress, fighting, and anger. Whatever you are blaming – even if it is your own behaviour – you are resisting. Allow, accept responsibility for it, and get back into the flow.

Any time you experience stress or tension, your body is sending you a message. You can accept your feelings and relax into them, or push back. You cannot find out what the message is if you continue feeling stressed out and tense. It is that simple.

Vulnerability and surrender are powerful tools to keep you in a non-resistant state. Resistance cannot survive alongside those vibrational qualities. Opening and softening, knowing you are supported and safe, dissolves resistance.

Resistance is also another form of denial. We can resist taking responsibility for our lives, so we justify ourselves and our actions by blaming someone or something for what is happening. I am sick because it runs in our mother's genes. I did not get that job because this company does not want to pay me what I am worth. And on, and on. War is resistance on a monumental scale. Entire nations deny culpability for their part in an issue, so decide to blame another country for their problems.

Much of society resists constantly. The collective refusal to take responsibility on deeply divisive issues supports the continuation of war, greed and power-over. If peace is an outcome you desire, accept responsibility for your part in the perpetuation of war, forgive yourself, and then release all resistance to war. Does that response feel counterintuitive in this moment? Do it anyway. It is a first step in healing some of the planet's deepest and most persistent wounds. Of course, you are healing ancient as well as modern wounds within yourself, too. It is the same process for everything. Do not be anti – war, poverty, hunger. Rather, be pro-peace, abundance, sustainability. That is how we will realise the loving change we wish to see in the world. It is that simple.

What you do, of course, is your choice. Always and all ways, your choice. Choose wisely. It is natural to feel resistance to aspects within this book. You might feel tense when it comes to letting go, to surrendering, to being vulnerable. It is okay. Your default setting is trying desperately to hold on to familiar patterns. Trust that as you shed light on what is no longer serving you, resistance to change will fall away. As you open and step away from resistance, you will find it easier to love deeper and tap into vibrations of healing. Resist nothing, and one day soon, you will rise above all the crazy, scary adventures, into your highest, most loving life. You will be an example for others who, when they are ready, will rise, too.

Soften and let go. You are safe to do so.

7.6 Mind Battle

Everything you are doing is in your mind. Catching your judgments, paying attention, and noticing how things are processed is all in your mind. As you focus and expand your awareness, it is in your mind. The fact that you have a mind along for the ride on this earthly experience is nothing short of divine.

Abusing this capacity in any way does not serve your highest purpose.

Every day we watch the push-pull of a system hell bent on being right, supporting an old story. The system continues to see human and animal life as expendable while exploiting a planet already in peril. How can this be? It is a reflection of our own mental conflict, a lack of accountability and responsibility, and a denial of our oneness. We create more by pushing against it all.

With regards to your personal transformation, it is important to know your distorted mind is going to fight for its survival. Our patterns and thoughts are well formed, deeply entrenched, and do not want to give up. They will resist your attempts to change. This battle is enforced in the world around you, too.

The depth of your distortions will dictate the degree to which your default setting will fight back. It is well trained, almost militaristic in fashion. Furthermore, your cellular memory will, at times, make it hard for you to stay in a loving state. For example, you may have been telling yourself a story about being fat and ugly for a really long time. As you do this work, one of your tasks is to feel radiantly beautiful. On an 'up' day, it is easy to feel wonderful, while on a 'down' day, your mind will be judging you, reminding you of how ugly you really are. Your thoughts will suggest you are stupid for trying to change, or thinking you could ever be beautiful. You might hear, "Who am I to feel good about myself?" And so on.

The distorted mind will run you in fear filled circles. This battle is one you must commit to holding your ground in. See these as the tricks your mind is playing on you. Stand strong, tapping into your loving, and aware state. Become like Gandalf the White, shedding your old grey cloak to stand in your new light-filled power against the darkness of old and destructive patterns. No longer are you going to play the victim of your own insidious thinking. You are, like Gandalf, going to plummet to your darkest, fiery depths, and rise as the true Wizard of Love that you are. BOOM!

It will be like that in your mind. You are going to feel low, icky, and sticky, even powerless, but you must not succumb. You must know that this battle will happen repeatedly until the darkest bits are exposed to the light. Remember, keep reminding yourself, that you are a wizard. Own your power and see yourself winning the most important battle you will ever fight – the one in your own mind.

I believe in your power, and see the light in your eyes. When in darkness, remember that the light will always prevail. Harry Potter defeated Voldemort, Frodo destroyed the ring, and you, too, will conquer your greatest fears. We're all in this together. Stay strong and just keep going.

Your loving life awaits you on the other side of your mind battles. Dig deep, grab your light sabre and be prepared, the distorted mind can strike when you least expect it. Stay grounded and hold to your vision of a loving new world.

Tell yourself you are epic, a superhero, because you are. You have come so far.

7.7 What To Expect

Expect to be more able to distance yourself from people and environments that do not feel good to you anymore. You should feel more grounded, and more empowered, able to adjust and deal with upheavals more calmly.

You should feel more in tune with your intuition and ready to follow through with its guidance. Maybe you have decided to leave your job, or move house. Perhaps you have decided to go travelling for a year to give yourself space and time to figure things out. You are establishing a much more fearless life, and so, are creating adventure and fun.

Your writing and new found intuitive abilities should be inspiring you. Maybe you have decided to start a blog, or give a weekly talk in your home town. Maybe you have started painting, or joined a dance course, just for fun.

You are breaking free from the mould and it feels good. Playfulness is returning to your life. Yes, you still get triggered and yes, you still sit with emotional waves and storms, but your emotions no longer scare you, and you are no longer beating yourself up when you are tired, sad, or angry. You are much better at allowing it all.

Expect to see longer stints of flow state, or at least, expect to be better at noticing when you are having fun and in a state of timelessness. You are getting much better at detaching from thoughts and generally feeling a whole lot lighter. Reversely, expect to be better at noticing when you are not in the flow. You should be paying closer attention to your stress and tension levels more instinctively and using all of your ammunition of breath, movement and meditation practices to combat your daily stress triggers with a powerful loving awareness. Now that you know stress, tension, and worrying needn't be normal, you are taking direct action to clear up your distorted mind and dissolve those painful patterns.

This is powerful and you know it, now, more than ever. Be proud of yourself for having the courage to face your demons and feel the depths of your pain.

You are dropping much deeper now with an expanding recognition of the tricks and games your distorted mind will try to play on you when it comes to dissolving your judgments and living in your state of flow. You will notice your resistance might feel quite intense, and yet the deeper you go you will feel more connected to your loving energy through your meditation and mindfulness practices.

Expect to be seeing more of the benefits of forgiveness like harmonious encounters and more relaxed and honest relationships. Expect to feel more loving toward all people, and yet selective about who you spend time with.

You are becoming more powerful with each passing day, and more enlightened with every conscious breath. Share your experiences, insights, and inspiration with The Tribe and keep going.

BONUS LESSON
Communication

Communication is a cornerstone for expanding harmoniously. Be aware that as you raise your vibrations, how you communicate will change. It is absolutely critical that you remain centred and in tune with your intuition when you are in communion with another human being.

You are not just listening with your ears now, but your entire energy field. It may be that you simply need to hold space for people as they express themselves. Verbal responses are not always necessary, while being fully present to another, is. If you are genuinely called to respond, make sure you are speaking from your heart. If someone reacts adversely to you, remember that is about them and where they are, not a direct reflection of you. On the other hand, if you catch yourself reacting adversely to, or being triggered emotionally by someone's behaviour, or words, own your feelings, withdraw from the situation and transform the energy that has arisen. Wait for that loving, feel good guidance, to flood in. This is the place where everybody wins.

If you notice people's eyes glazing over when you speak, that usually means you have lost them. Most of us have experienced this at one time or another. In regards to the transformative material in this guide, there are likely going to be those who are not ready to hear what you are saying about it, which means they are not willing at this time to look more deeply within themselves to overcome certain issues. It is perfectly okay. Remember everyone is walking their own path, and you must respect that. Forcing your views onto people does not change them. Even worse, it can create more resistance in you, and in them. It is a sure sign of your ego grasping and arrogance. Your practice is to forgive, and let go.

Practice remaining present and lovingly responsible in all your communication. This is key in building long lasting, ever blossoming, and truly nurturing relationships. Be yourself and let other people be themselves. Collectively, our communication must change. Trust your vibes, be willing to let go of people that are no longer resonating with you, and expect to meet people who 'get' you. Your vibes will attract your tribe. Have no doubt about it.

Choose to be around people who make you laugh, who let you cry, and who permission you to shine your light. These people are your soul family. Celebrate them as you continue to celebrate yourself.

Exercises

Step 7. Living in the Flow

Exercise A.

When was the last time you got impatient? Describe what happened in a short paragraph. Be prepared to share.

Exercise B.

Name 3 thoughts that don't feel good. For example: My dad doesn't love me. I'm a lousy cook. I'm too fat to wear that. He only likes me when I'm drunk.

Be honest, this might be a tough exercise for some of you. Be prepared to share and discuss.

Exercise C.

What triggers you? Write down one example of people, places and things that trigger you. Be prepared to discuss.

Exercise D.

Name one thing you do that brings you into a timeless state. Pay attention to what you are doing, the people you are around, and the places you find yourself when you feel this time-lessness. Do more of it. No matter how counterintuitive this might feel in comparison to your default setting. Joy is your job. Full stop.

Explain how you are creating more flow in your life? Be prepared to discuss.

Exercise E.

Name an exercise in this guide that brought up resistance. Please be honest and be prepared to discuss.

Exercise F.

Create your superhero persona. What's your superhero name? What's your superpower? Can you see her? Make a drawing or write it down. Be prepared to share.

Step 8. Willing and Open

8.1 Willingness

If you are not willing to bend, you will break.

Willingness, like surrender and vulnerability, is a tremendous aid to your growth. Being in a state of readiness means you are always prepared to dissolve the conditions, constructs, and conventions of the old collective agreements of this world, and transform energy that no longer serves the masses. Willingness ushers you to keep going and growing.

As you become more aware of the subtleties of your judgments, limiting beliefs, and assumptions, you will begin to feel more in alignment and in love, more connected to who you feel yourself to truly be. Your willingness to accept these changes with gratitude, is important in your continued expansion and ever-evolving creative journey.

This guide is a means of enabling you to look at yourself from as many different angles as possible and to soften away from any rigidity, limitations, and falsehoods. Your willingness to shed your limitations is a testament to the work you are doing, and it never ends.

You might have great success in peeling back a judgment, or in manifesting more love in your life which is wonderful. However, the work can sometimes feel like you are swinging back and forth.

Imagine facing a bridge. You take three steps over the bridge and suddenly jump back, afraid. Next attempt, you take five steps across the bridge, feel alone suddenly, and then jump back. And on and on until you get to the other side. This is what it can feel like, so always be willing to take another step. Do not give up.

Each step in this guidebook is like a permission slip, gently ushering you to something more. You must be willing to face all the fears you have created along the way and have faith that love and abundance lives on the other side of the bridge. It does, even if you have not realised it yet. Next time, once you take three steps, instead of jumping all the way back to the start, take half a step back and then be willing to take the next step. Be kind to yourself no matter what you do.

This is why kindness is so important. You are a pioneer, breaking new frontiers. This is profound work you are doing, so find a place within yourself where there is no time or space for you to be hard on yourself. Catch yourself being hard on yourself. Do not be afraid to love all of the hardness, all of the judgments, and all of the unwillingness. You will soon see it all with more love and clarity.

Resistance is an unwillingness to change. Your harsh judgments against yourself and others is an unwillingness to let go of a painful story and to drop your arrogance. Willingness is the ability to throw your hands up in the air, surrender it all, put an end to the complaining, and forget that you know anything at all.

Be willing to change. Be willing to remember your innocence again and that childlike curiosity that came before you labelled and defined everything. Be willing to play again and to remember how to have fun. In a willing state, you harness a far greater capacity for learning in your adult form. Be willing to use your mind in ways that you never imagined possible up to this point. Be willing to surprise yourself.

Be willing to accept that everything is happening in your mind's awareness. If there are rigid elements in your mind, stuck on a wavelength of, "I know this. I know that. This is how things should be!" then you are not willing and open for new possibilities. In that moment, you are unwilling to detach from that limiting thought because you are trying desperately to be right. But do not worry, once you notice it, you can change it. You just have to be willing to.

Being willing opens you to the fact that you are not in control of everything, and that you really know nothing for sure. You are, however, prepared to accept how you feel from moment to moment. Surrender, be willing, surrender and be willing. On it goes.

What you are doing is all part of the merging process; that you merge your perception of an individual identity into a unified identity. Your one Self is actually merging with all that you perceive. You are totally responsible and consciously willing to love it ALL.

When willing to recognise that you are one with the other, if something comes into your awareness that you do not like, you need not reject it. Do not push against it. See it and be willing to gently release it. You are the observer and observed. You are willing to detach from everything you thought you were and create something entirely new and shiny. Be willing to receive your shiny new self. As you deepen your loving connection to your highest self, be willing to believe you can fulfil your wildest dreams.

Be willing to let lack, fear, and worry dissolve. Do it for you and for the entire human race. You have decided you want to change so be willing to take the leap. Be ready to deal with every challenge you face along the way.

There is a cool saying from Kundalini yoga master, Yogi Bhajan who says, "Understand through compassion or you will misunderstand the times." This is a prevailing truth for our time. If you are in anger, judgment, attack, or defence mode, you are not seeing clearly. Indeed, you are hiding from your deepest and truest self. Owning your energy, becoming fully empowered and responsible, is choosing compassion every time.

Remember this saying whenever you are fighting with someone, or feeling anger, even if you think it is for a good reason. Choose to transform your pain and dissolve the anger until you can feel compassion for the person, the situation, and yourself.

Be willing to let go of what you think is right for you and everyone else, and instead, simply be willing to learn. As you learn, be willing to receive the gifts that this expansive, abundant, and infinite life has in store for you. Be willing to change the entire story. You once believed in lack, you once believed you were undeserving, unworthy, and not enough. Be willing to change all that. Be willing to live your wildest dreams.

If you are reading this book, consider yourself awakened. Consider yourself doing service to humanity by connecting the mind to the heart, integrating higher wisdom into your body, and dissolving dense distortions. Your work is rippling out and the waves just keep getting better.

Your loving life awaits, if you are willing to keep going. Please do. Life is willing to assist you and so am I.

You are everything you seek, be willing to remember.

8.2 Open to Receive

Now that you are well and truly on your way, as you establish your new foundation for living through ongoing conscious transformation, you absolutely must be open to receiving more love and abundance. This might seem silly to you. You might think, "Why would I not be open to such good stuff?" Let me explain.

You are getting better at riding out emotional storms, waves and triggers, and in so doing, you are embodying more love, harmonising your relationships, and remembering how to enjoy life again. Your daily meditation practice is offering you greater clarity, and you feel better connected to your intuition. Your ability to take greater responsibility for your life is also expanding. Onwards and upwards you climb.

However, remember whenever you complain, moan, blame or defend, you are powerless and closed. Your own light is being masked by your judgments. Own the judgment, transform the old pattern, and remember your light.

The greatest gift you can give this world, is your light, your joy, your love. Once you tap into that, be ready to receive some goodness. Keep opening up to more joy and excitement. Imagine it! Drop deep into your own fearlessness, your own truly loving and compassionate heart, and radiate that vibration so that you can see the world through Love's eyes. By opening to new possibilities, adventure, action, and even weirdness, you keep the momentum going.

Keep reminding yourself that there is nothing outside of you to fix, there's nothing outside of you to get or to gain. You are simply opening doors within your own mind. As you continue to open up, expect your reality to open up to you, too, which can mean receiving insights and ideas, more friends, more money, or anything at all that comes into your reality. Be open and willing enough to receive it all.

You are actually always receiving. Why? Because you are always creating, always manifesting something. Whether it be lack, or some form of abundance, you are always receiving your own creative vibrational output. It is all one and the same. How you are relating to it, or how you are reacting to what is coming your way, depends on your awareness. In other words, if your default setting has you accustomed to receiving lack, then you have to get used to receiving abundance. Being grateful for the awareness, helps a lot. Gratitude sends out positive energy which further expands your desire for abundance. Who needs a state of lack? You certainly do not.

Be open to the process shape-shifting for you. You might be inspired to develop an ability you have. This is that permission slip to, again, be flexible and see where it might lead. Be willing, also, to drop any endeavour completely if at some point you feel it is not for you, which is really the greatest permission slip of all. There's nothing outside of you, no one person, school, course, manual, or institution more powerful than you. You are the only true power in your reality because you are the only one having the experience within your own consciousness.

That, my friends, is a deep recognition: That you are all that is. If there are areas of your life that feel limited, that cause anger or elicit frustration, it is you. It is always you. You are triggering yourself to wake yourself up. Keep at it. Breathe deeply and be open to change. It is exciting, and so worthwhile.

Be open to having breakthroughs, incredible insights, and life-changing ideas.

Life is an incredible paradox. We all want things and convince ourselves having them will make us happy, to bring us what we think we need to be satisfied. Yet, as we break it down, it is not even those things that bring us joy. It is the simple things such as feeling connected, and loved. Be open to feeling completely connected in every moment. Feel the love in your heart for yourself and let it radiate from you. Be open to slowing down enough so that you can enjoy these simple things; your friends, your solitude, and nature. Let the ordinary become extraordinary, and fall back in love with life. Be open to believing that Earth is an enchanted kingdom. Be open to believing in fairy tales and let your fairy light shine!

As you strengthen your resolve and persist in your practices to live fearlessly, the emotions you experience may intensify. You are strengthening new patterns and your vibrations are shifting to match them. Respond as you would for excitement, ecstasy, or bliss. These new vibrations might be a bit scary, especially if you have been feeling low, but they are part of the process. Ground them into your body so they embed deeply. Let them imprint on you and allow your body to take on more and more light.

Can you see at this point, how cyclical the process is? Your awareness expands as you consciously own and transform dense emotional patterns. When a block has been removed from your energy frequency, suddenly, even the so-called simplest things, become beautiful. These experiences increase your gratitude. Remaining open to receive it all lifts you into higher and higher vibrations. And on it goes.

Your energetic field is expanding, and those things that you once thought scary are falling away. Stay open to receive love and let it multiply within. Raise yourself up with your own creative connection; use the force.

Your light is shining brighter by the day.

8.3 Fearless Love

Fearless love is about making a choice to consciously face every perceived fear from a loving place within you. Your beautiful heart connects you to feelings, and to every experience you have. You radiate your entire vibrational field outward from that heart space. It is your creation station! Meanwhile, your mind allows you to perceive an external reality.

From the perspective of the distorted mind, everything is random and separate from everything else. Once you connect your mind to the feeling centre of the heart, you are able to recognise you are "other", too.

In order to dissolve perceived fears, you must commit to practicing fearless love. Some might call this self-love, but I am not going to use the expression here because I do not want to confuse it with behaviours that end up demonstrating themselves in the form of arrogance, power over, or superiority, which have nothing at all to do with love. I want to steer away from the mentality of, "Well, because I did this it makes me better than you."

Fearless love is holistic, permanent, and unwavering eternal love. It is the love that loves all of creation's emanations, the light and the dark. It is the fearless love within you that can love the fear itself. It is the fearless love within you that cries when it sees pain in the world. It is your fearless love that brought you here to this point on your journey.

Fearless love sees all the violence, all the anger, all the war, and wants you to love it all away. When, through love, you deepen your connection to your expanded, or multi-dimensional self, your higher self, spirit or soul, you integrate that spiritual essence into your physical body. That essential self then radiates love through you, creating a new world.

When we commit to being in union with our universal selves, we are helping humanity to collectively 'sort it out'. As we continue on that path, more answers will be revealed and new creations will continue to clear paths where needed. When loving fearlessly, there is a deepening of the commitment to raising the vibration of the entire collective. It is important to recognise you are not doing this work for the singular you. You are not just doing this work to get ahead in the world, to make more money, or buy a bigger house. This is divine work - you could even say that it is pre-agreed, already written - for the whole.

Now, the only real work left to do is within us. By igniting the divine spark within each individual, they can remember who they really are. We must give ourselves, and all others, permission to access the insights inherent in higher vibrational states of being. Basically, we just have to love each other, no matter what.

As you increase your love vibes, you will become more aware of the varying wavelengths, or you could say, varying energies within each individual. Every encounter is an opportunity to expand your love. Watch carefully, though. Catch any judgments, or resistances.

Your ability to love it all fearlessly is powerful and integral to further transformation. Remember Step 7, and be like a Jedi.

Be the wizard or a superhero. Liken yourself to something beyond what you think possible of, or for, yourself. You are magnificent whether you believe it or not.

Somewhere, deep within, we know that love conquers all regardless of what people choose to vibrate, or choose to think about. Love is always there waiting patiently for us. It is the container supporting all of creation. Nothing is created without love. We would not see the atrocity and anger around us without love. Perhaps that is the very reason some choose to push love away. Not you, though. You are wholeheartedly committed to living a fearless life by loving it all. Ask yourself, "What do you want to create while you are here? What do you want to experience?" You can create from a place of powerlessness or loving purpose. It is that simple.

At any time you can choose to ignore how you are feeling, or blame your external reality, but now you know that by doing that you would be choosing to create more of the same. External conditions cannot affect you unless you let them. From this standpoint, you have the power to do anything. You live in your own virtual reality, creating it from within your own feeling imagination. It all comes down to what you are buying into as "real" and what you are choosing to see. If there is stuff in your world you do not want to see anymore, you must choose to see something different. That different will come from your own imagination.

Keep diving deep into the fearlessness within you; that unconditional, totally expanded place until you are able to love it all fearlessly. From this place within yourself, you can clear a once muddled and distorted channel to bring forth your most divine creation. You are cleaning up your vibrational mess and creating the most awesome imaginative vision you have access to, to live it now!

Fearless love is what it is all about. It is digging deep, grabbing hold of that love, allowing it to expand within your being and then fearlessly releasing it to the entire universe. Believe that your heart's call is being answered, and that your dreams and prayers for a loving world are being heard. Believe and know, too, that as you expand your conscious awareness, so too do you expand the entire collective. We are one, and as you experience greater loving abundance, you give others access to the same.

You have some really juicy work ahead of you. You are amazing. You are fearless, even if you don't know it yet.

Remember, we all make mistakes! As explorers and creators, we are here to learn. There is no need to pretend anymore. No one really knows what they are doing. Everyone is just making it up as they go along. You can too, just make it fun.

Relax. And, keep going. You are beautiful. Keep shining!

BONUS LESSON
Body Love

The best way to "get" the body you want, is to totally and unconditionally LOVE THE BODY YOU HAVE. This is not about vanity or, as you already know, superiority. It is not about fitting into cookie-cutter media images. You chose your body for a reason and if you hate it, it is going to hate you right back.

****

A personal theme of mine, for most of my life, was loathing my body. I can remember, at eight years old, looking in the mirror and not liking what I saw. I did not look like the beautiful women on TV and so, I told myself I was disgusting; I was eight!

By the time I turned thirteen, I was anorexic. At fifteen, after hitting puberty, I became bulimic. Bulimia turned into obsessive exercise and food control. In my late teens and early twenties, the distorted views I had of myself led to excessive partying. I was in deep pain and denial, fluctuating between starvation and excess. My entire life was spiralling out of control.

On my thirtieth birthday, broke, homeless, alone, and still hating my body, I'd had enough. So, I dove in, fearlessly. I took full responsibility for everything and firmly decided that my life was going to change once and for all.

I began to diligently reprogram my inner dialogue around my body. I would stare at myself in the mirror, usually in tears, and say to myself, "I am not here to judge you anymore". I would caress my skin, and gently tell my body, "I love you. Thank you."

The physical transformation did not happen overnight, but took approximately two years. I did not control my food, because I desired total liberation. I ate whatever I wanted whenever I wanted it, with a new inner dialogue, which said that whatever I desired was perfect for my perfect body. I imagined how I desired my body to look with an inner knowing that, that was my divine form. I sat many a morning and evening in meditation crying tears caused from the painful memories of a lonely little girl eating whole containers of ice cream and then hiding the evidence. I wrapped my arms around my belly and told myself, "You are safe to breathe. You are safe to take up space. You are allowed to be exactly who are." And the tears kept coming.

Miraculously, over time and with a diligent inner commitment to the process, my body began to change shape. I started to feel free and happy in my form again. And, I know I am now free of that burden and can live happily ever after in my body. So can you.

****

Begin your "Body Love" journey NOW. Love it, caress it, and tend to your painful memories, by facing them fearlessly. Love that child unconditionally. Hug and nurture the child who deserves love.

And with it all, have some fun. Dress up. Take time every day to give yourself a kiss; this is a love affair after all, one you are going to have with yourself. And I do not care how cheesy you think it sounds. I thought so, too, for a long time. But, if I could go back and tell my eight year old self that she was beautiful, and perfect, I would have saved myself a whole lot of pain.

Do not wait. LOVE ALL OF YOU NOW. Every little detail, every little, or big curve. You are a gorgeous, sexy, fully alive divine and sacred being. Own it. By doing so, you will leave any doubters, or haters, squinting in your light trail.

Love is the most powerful tool for lasting change. Use it. Blaze on you sexy Goddesses and Gods!

8.4 Change

Change is the only constant. It is happening all the time. You are undergoing radical transformation by reading the content in this guide, so it is safe to say, you are changing.

Top Tip: Practice fearless love in the face of all fear, including fear of change!

You may start to notice you are not really fitting into your old world anymore. As you continue to deepen your connection to love, your vibration will shift dramatically at different stages of your process. This is awesome! Just be prepared. Know that it may be a little uncomfortable or really uncomfortable at times. No matter what, you are always growing, changing, learning and expanding in love and higher vibrations.

You are changing, and through this change, you are creating a better world. At first, it may feel scary because your mind is conditioned to believe change is bad. As you continue to harmonise your frequency to your new patterns of response, your world, the people around you, your home, maybe even your working environment, will naturally begin to change.

195

Disclaimer: If your intuition is telling you to do something such as leave a job, move house, stop hanging with certain friends, become a vegetarian, or leave a partner, for example, and you are unwilling to follow through with the changes your intuition is asking you to make, you will stagnate and your most challenging emotional behavioural patterns will escalate. You will halt the transformational process, and remain bound to less than desirable illusions.

Whatever choices you make are acceptable. There is no judgment here. This Step, however, requires you to follow through with what your intuition is asking of you, which may require burning through some pretty profound fears, and barriers. When you do make those changes and voice your truth, you stand in your essential power, and, as scary as it may feel, it will lead you to a more positive state of being, even though it is highly likely to bring up pain, initially. Think of it like jumping into a cold pool. The quicker you do it, the quicker it is over and you can enjoy your swim.

It is only after you take that leap of faith that things start to show up for you, big and small. As long as you remain open and willing to take action, which means moving in a direction so as to become the person you desire to be, then, quite simply, over a period of time, your old reality will fall away and you will begin to see a new one unfold. Just. Like. That. You do have to believe it with every fibre of your being, though. Complete faith.

In your new world, you will notice the beauty of a delicate flower, the sunshine making the leaves of the trees shine more brightly. You will notice that people around you are happier, and you will be having more fulfilling conversations with not only your friends, but random strangers, because you now know that everyone is a loving friend. You will begin to draw in this new reality and your expansion will become exponential. You will actually feel the momentum.

Be proud of yourself for the work that you have done. Do not shrug it off with, "Oh no, it is probably just the weather." No. It is you. It is always you, so own your creation. Are you starting to have more consistent good days? Are you feeling more energy? It is you, so give yourself the credit you deserve. You are transforming patterns that once made you feel tired and depressed. You are the one creating the new now. It is a big deal. It is deep work and it is amazing. Give yourself credit.

From within you there is a constant energy exchange. You are learning to ground higher frequency into a human form. As with cause and effect, as your frequency changes so does your world. Simple. You just have to be courageous enough to let it change and then, live it. In the words of Gandhi, "You must be the change you wish to see in the world."

Real change occurs when you feel it. Really feel it. This is what it means to embody something. It is no longer words you are throwing around. You become the words, so you cannot talk about being all love, and then turn around and rage at the system for being corrupt. That does nothing helpful.

Inner work is action, a tangible experience you are having inside your own awareness. It is you working with consciousness. As you continue, you ground your changes, those awesome visions, deep into your body. From there, you send that energy out from your heart as far as you can imagine. In these sacred inner moments, you are calling in the new. You are changing the world with the power of your imagination! Make it sweet!

Never forget you are unique. There is no one right way to be, quite the opposite is true. There are infinite ways of being. We, as a collective, are choosing to experience a perceived finite timeline. Regardless of what you think, all of it is still an illusion of your mind. Your awakening is you, seeing through the illusion of form and time, into greater light, love, and clarity. Shine your light in whatever form it comes! You are here. You are of value because you breathe. You exist because you are having an experience of existence.

In the words of Michael Jackson, "Take a look at yourself and make a change". When you do this, things are going to change. BIG TIME.

Let it be.

8.5 Overflowing Generosity

"Unless someone like you cares a whole awful lot, nothing is going to get better. It is not." Dr. Seuss

If you want to experience infinite, overflowing abundance in your life, start giving, a lot. This Step has less to do with material possessions or money, though it certainly does include these things. Overflowing generosity is to do with your energy, your time, and most importantly, your love. It is time to start caring in a really big way, because you absolutely can make a difference. We all can. And, we must.

The fact is, your life will only improve when you start caring about the world around you which includes life in all its forms. It includes this planet, too. Caring does not mean coming from a place of self-sacrifice or righteousness. True caring is an act of love. Everything will align and your dreams will come true when you stop moaning and start giving.

Under the illusion of lack there is often fear attached to giving because it looks like something must be lost. If I give something to someone else then I am losing that object. On an energetic level, giving is receiving. The more you give, the more you get. Your giving is a way to exponentially expand your creative pulling power, i.e., the power you have to pull in your desires.

There appears to be a wide spread energy of entitlement leaking throughout western cultures. Perhaps it has to do with chasing the promise of the American Dream, or, mainstream media's version of success. Reality television shows spread this entitled mind-set by glamorising stupidity and superficiality. It seems nothing is too disgusting if it gets you on TV. None of these messages support generosity, only greed. This vibration is detrimental to our human energy field and so we must transform it.

What will bring you lasting joy? Getting yourself to a place where you feel you are overflowing with love and generosity. A place where smiles come easily, and are given to everyone you come across. A place where it is effortless for you to reach into your pocket and share some cash with someone who needs it. And a place where you wouldn't think twice before giving a friend in need, or even a stranger, a hug. It is the simple things. Only your old conditioning would have you believe anything different. All the clothes, and money and drugs in the world, are not going to make you happy. Those are temporary fixes. But you are changing all of it. Right here. Right now. How?

You stopped watching TV and started contributing more simply by tapping into your creative imagination. You started seeking out joy and doing whatever you need to do to increase that state. In fact, you desire your joy levels to be so high that every step you take uplifts humanity. You have to stop pretending you want to be like Kim Kardashian, or Paris Hilton, because you do not. You want to be you in the fullness of who you are and who you are meant to become.

And here is a surprise. The reason many celebs appear happy is because many of them are. They are themselves, fully. And I am not dissing them, I honour them as beautiful sacred beings doing their thing. Personally, I am more aligned with people like Emma Thompson, and Leonardo DiCaprio; celebrities who are stepping up and actually talking about stuff that matters to the entire planet. But each of us has a path.

So, check in with yourself. If you are still worrying and complaining about not having enough, go back to Step 1 and get grateful. It does not matter how dire your situation looks. There is always another way to look at, to see, everything. And, if you find you are still trying for something "out there", you need to look deeper within yourself.

I do not doubt that many will be triggered by the mere mention of money. Everyone has their money assumptions. A state of trying is a state of fear, because it comes from the feeling of not being enough. It is time to break these chains. You are enough! You are more than enough! You are deserving! Stop looking for the answers out there.

A recognition that you are creating this hamster wheel of lack has to happen. There has to be some sort of "A-ha" moment for you to reverse the cycle. Again, this guide is intended to do that for you by helping you pull yourself back into the creator seat and realign yourself with your loving purpose. Doing so will bring you joy, love, and abundance beyond your wildest dreams. If you intend to move with love, the resources you need will appear. That is enough. If you continue to make money an excuse for why you cannot do this, or that, you will only continue to limit yourself.

If you still think abundance is about the size of your bank balance, it is not. Like everything else, it is a feeling. Abundance is an overflowing joy and gratitude for life. If you only focus on increasing your bank balance, then what? You are still going to want more. Abundance is more joy, more happiness, more excitement, and more love which all comes from inside you.

No longer is it about accumulating money so that one person can feel more powerful than another. This is about integrity with the totality, and indeed, truly knowing that every single human being has the potential, and right, to live in infinite abundance. It all starts in you.

****

HIGH LEVEL VISION: If you are committed to moving in a direction where you are one day completely free from a distorted economic structure, then really, it is about us collectively dissolving the "not enough" energy within human consciousness. Your success in living fearlessly has to do with how clearly you reframe your relationship with your entire life, which is all in you. And there are only two choices: Give or Take. Love or Lack.

Recognise that anytime you are afraid of giving, you are limiting yourself. In that moment begin to shift your focus to contribution, and adding value, rather than allowing fear to say there is something you will miss out on if you give. Think deeply, truly listen and honour your heart's call because it is leading lead you to ultimate abundance whether you are consciously aware of it, or not.

202

8.6 What To Expect

You have made it this far. Well done! And, thank you. You are engaging your star power and are having a positive impact on the world. By now, you are seeing the results of your manifestation power. Your self-mastery is in sight. Your inner work is changing your perspective and with this new outlook, there comes greater ease, more flow, and more joy. Your eyes and ears are open for signs, serendipities, and coincidences.

You are becoming more aware of themes in your life, and specific challenges. You are rising above them with more and more success. Expect to be called on to share insights and wisdom.

Whenever you think to, but especially when you start to see fun new stuff showing up, applaud yourself.

With all the new fun you are having, keep it grounded, and continue the work. Notice those subtle triggers. If you start to see some of your manifestations show up, just make sure to keep that so-called ego of yours in-check. Beware of thoughts like, "it won't last" or "who are you to feel so good?" Or, on the flip side, "Ha! I showed them!"

Notice any guilt you feel about feeling wonderful, or around good things you have created. Transform the guilt every time it pops up. Ground the excitement if it starts to run away with you.

Expect odd things to occur, too. Know they only appear weird. Maybe you think you are getting really good at manifesting when out of nowhere you have a car accident. You feel totally blindsided. Be pleased. This is most definitely a sign. Your higher self is saying, "I am here for you, just slow down and listen."

You have always been manifesting. Everyone is always manifesting. The difference is that now, you are aware you are manifesting, so choose to do so on a higher vibrational frequency.

Be proud of yourself. Keep loving one another, and reaching out. Support one another through this process because the broader your love becomes, the easier the clearing will become for everyone.

Have fun. Keep going. You are amazing.

BONUS LESSON
Touch

There are studies out there that tell us that a twenty second hug releases "feel good" hormones in our bodies. Hug more.

There are definitely cultures who touch more than others. Of late, we have begun to fear touch, almost demonising it as possible perversion. Obviously, on a certain level, it can be, but touch is sacred and should be treated that way. So, hug your friends and family more. Heck, hug strangers if you are called to do so. Collectively, we need to re-integrate touch as the beautiful and healing thing it is, not something to be feared. Love is a kind embrace. Love is holding someone when they are struggling.

Touch is a good and necessary thing. It absolutely does not have to lead to sex. Be clear with your boundaries, stay connected to your inner guidance, and when called to hug, or hold someone, do it. If you feel you need a hug, ask for it. Touch is sacred, and we need to reclaim that for our own well-being. Go for massages with therapists who resonate with you. Be loving and kind toward your own body, in an intimate way. This will lead you into greater compassion for yourself and others.

If you are guided to reach out and open up the conversation with The Fearless Life Tribe, please do. This is a massive topic, but not one we are going to delve into deeply just yet.

Sending you all a great big hug!

Step 8. Willing and Open

Exercise A.

Where are you finding it impossible to bend? Where are you still feeling difficulty and/or stress in your life? What changes still feel too scary to make? Where are you not taking responsibility for how you feel? What or whom are you still attacking?

This is a tough exercise. You are going to write down a list of all the areas in your life that are still triggering you in a negative way. Simply be honest and objective.

Be prepared to discuss.

Exercise B.

In exercise 8A you listed all the challenges you are still facing. Now, list all your breakthroughs. Let yourself feel really good about your progress no matter how obvious or subtle the experience. Write it all down and be prepared to discuss.

Exercise C.

This is mirror work and some regard it as powerfully transformative. You are going to stare at yourself in the mirror, every day for 10 seconds and say to yourself, "I love and accept myself exactly as I am."

Write down any fears or concerns that come up during this exercise and be willing to discuss.

Exercise D.

Name one for each question. Be prepared to discuss.

1. What inner changes have you felt?

2. What external changes have you noticed?

Exercise E.

Go through your closet and cupboards. Put together a good sized bag of your clothes and/or household objects and give it away. While you're at it, de-clutter and throw away any items you have totally forgotten about.

How does this make you feel?

Step 9. Take Responsibility & Claim Your Star Power

9.1 Responsibility

"The price of greatness is responsibility." Winston Churchill

It is your life, no one else's. This Step will help guarantee your greatness in living an awesome life. If you do not take responsibility for your life, you are doomed to repeating the same painful patterns. So, this is an all important step if you want real change in your world. No one can do this for you. It is not possible. So, are you ready to claim your star power?

Having come this far, you have a responsibility to commit yourself to the continuation of this process. You will start to get glimpses of your star power and you will be shown how to use it. Through owning your junk, you will be guided in how to continue to release it and then, how to shine your divine essence onto every area of your life.

"You cannot escape the responsibility of tomorrow by evading it today." Abraham Lincoln

It is your responsibility to feel good and to choose better, more loving thoughts. It is your responsibility to break through the barriers, the limitations, the judgments, the fears and the illusion of separateness. Your freedom is your responsibility.

It is your responsibility to show a way for others, leading by example. Not through what you say, not through what you do necessarily, but through the vibration, the energies you emit and radiate from your heart. It is your responsibility to start to play your part in creating a new collective social agreement. We all play our part in this and, you hold the key to your own unlocking. The responsibility is within you to go deeper within yourself and unlock the vision you carry for your new world.

"Let us not seek to fix the blame for the past. Let us accept our own responsibility for the future." John F. Kennedy

It is your responsibility to spread happiness and leave people better off than when they met you, simply by choosing to love them, no matter what.

When you start to take responsibility for all your feelings, really cool things will start to happen and you will be shown ways to stay inspired; all from within your own infinite intelligence.

It is your responsibility to step in and help others when you are called to do so. It is your responsibility to be generous and kind and loving. It is your responsibility to clean up your mind, so that you can share your light with others.

"Most people do not really want freedom, because freedom involves responsibility, and most people are frightened of responsibility." Sigmund Freud

It is your responsibility to love every part of yourself; the ugliness, the pain, the fear, all of it. It is your responsibility to own it and love it.

You are shedding layer upon layer of anxiety and conflict in your mind about who you are, about why you are here. Ask yourself questions and expect to get answers. Whichever answer feels best, it is closer to your truth, so go with that one. It is your responsibility to get to know who you are.

It is your responsibility to let go of everything you think so you can feel your way into something more, a greater part of you that is timeless and effortlessly miraculous. There you will find your gifts and they will inspire you. They are going to feel exciting, and real even if no one else believes in them.

In accepting responsibility for your life, you are free to let go of everyone else's burdens, all of the ties to the world of separation and fear and control and domination. You are free to hang out with your highest self. Let yourself show up in life so that life can show up for you.

"A hero is someone who understands the responsibility that comes with his freedom." Bob Dylan

Being responsible is where the "greats" hang out; choose to be one of them. Choose to shine light into the darkness, while loving it. That darkness is a part of you too; but you are not going to be its slave any longer. Now, you are choosing to take charge of your life and to focus diligently on your own light.

210

No longer are you going to blame your parents, the governments, or the banks for your problems. You are going to take responsibility and transform resistant, blaming energies into cooperative energies determined to see only solutions.

You are Fearless. You are a Master. You are a Leader. Believe it.

Remember: In your willingness you will find your guides, friends, and allies. In your openness you will be forgiven for all past pain and grievances. Nothing you have ever done is being judged by anyone else but you. Own it. Love it and then, let it go. You can.

9.2 Diligence

Transformation requires diligence. You have been diligent so far, so keep going.

In the distorted mind of the system, we talk about work as labour, right? It is laborious, tedious and hard. We need to change the meaning of this word. Work is really your loving and inspired contribution to the world. You are not a slave. If you think work is hard, then you are a slave to an externally perceived authority. As you become responsible, you are remembering that you are the only authority in your perception.

Why are you doing what you are doing? Go deep. Ask yourself questions. Pay attention. What comes up? Be honest. If you can't find a good enough reason why you are doing what you are doing, then find other things to do. Ideally, stuff that feels fun and easy to you. What gets you excited? What makes you feel passion? What makes you feel good? Do more of that and be willing to let go of everything else.

Redefine the word work. For "work" to become easy and enjoyable, you gotta find your flow. You gotta know thyself. When you are flipping the world's mind-set, the idea of work gets flipped too. The reason it might look to you that there is so much "work" to be done "out there", is actually because there is so much work to be done inside of you. You can choose freedom or choose to stay on the hamster wheel of the rat race and keep thinking that, that is all there is or, "It's just the way things are". Stop making excuses.

It is totally cool if the rat race is still fun to you, but if the endless turning wheel does not feel good to you anymore, then you need to get off it, get grounded and decide where you want to go instead.

There's nothing mechanical to do that is all an illusion, because it is all already done. The only work left to do is within you. To expand the frequencies that feel good to you and dissolve the ones that do not.

Being diligent, just means keep going.

****

Okay. So, you are taking responsibility, well done! You are starting to feel pretty awesome and powerful and you are looking good. You are feeling really on top of this material and things are consistently feeling sweet. It feels like you are done, you have arrived. You are there. Then one day, you are sitting at a coffee shop and someone walks past you and you notice yourself pass a sly judgment. "If she wasn't eating those fries, she'd probably be thinner." Busted! Brutal, right? The distorted mind is super sneaky! Pay attention in those moments. As soon as a judgment is spotted, look at it, own it, harmonise it by sending that person you just judged some love. Apply the healing Band-Aid of forgiveness and move on.

****

Be diligent in reassessing your need to achieve. You know that if that kind of striving and grasping delivered, the world would be sorted by now. Be diligent in dropping the belief you need to achieve material stuff, or some particular level on the ladder, and do what makes you feel great, instead. The stuff you actually want will show up faster that way.

Gaining clarity through your persistence is part of the process. As we know, the system we live within can only survive through our collective agreement. If we unveil the dark illusion of separateness, we shine light on that darkness. You are that light. Once you see beyond the illusion, your love-light can lead the way for others, too. It is happening at this very moment. Do not doubt.

Be diligent, not arrogant. It seems to be a common pitfall in early spiritual practice. You start a new thing, be it yoga, or a new no-sugar diet, etc., and think, "This is it. This is the thing. I have got it now. It is going to sort me out!" In no time, you hear yourself saying, "Why yes, I have been practicing yoga for many weeks and I am basically enlightened." Or, you turn your nose up at a piece of cake your niece has baked. "Disgusting! Sugar is the devil! Get it away from me!" which makes your niece cry and feel bad for sharing.

These examples may sound ridiculous to you, but let's get real here, your mind IS totally and utterly ridiculous, so let's have fun with it, which can make the idea of diligence fun, too. None of the suggestions in this guide have to do with levels, or rightness. I am touching on issues that resonate deeply with my own transformation but remain fully aware that there are many, many ways to enrich your unique humanness.

If this, or any part of this process resonates, which means it feels good and makes sense to you, then, it is designed and meant for you. The content of this book is about love – the fearless kind. If the message gels, muster the courage to let your life change.

People talk about "hard work paying off", so people keep working hard. They are miserable, but keep going because they tell themselves, "one day it will pay off. It just has to!" The thing is, the payoff they seek does not come from hard work. It comes when they believe they deserve the pay off. Besides, life is not about the payoffs, it is not about being recognised or getting attention. Life is about moments. Life is about Love. Or, life is about whatever you want it to be about.

The clearer you become, the more light you will shine for others. Keep reminding yourself of this truth. As you transform more and more heavy energies, you will naturally embody more light, becoming a beacon for higher vibrations. Can you see yourself that way? Imagine, you as the shining star.

Everything is made up of light particles, or star stuff. The light particles organise themselves in many different forms such as galaxies, solar systems, planets, and us. Tiny as they may be, this star stuff is our beginning.

The spiral is a classic pattern in the universe. That is one way energy flows. The other is the wave. We vibrate, are never static, and move in the same outward and upward spiral pattern, just as Earth moves around Sun. We experience light flooding our awareness in waves. And on and on. Ever flowing, ever changing. Ever evolving. With each cycle we gain more tools to help in our release of that which no longer serves us. Very scientific.

If you have been behaving, or vibrating, on a certain frequency that is less than desirable, you need to know that you can change that behaviour. Furthermore, you are safe to do so. If you are scared of your power, however, diligence will mean nothing to you. You must come to trust the unknown and believe in magic.

The gentle nudging of your loving intuition, your heart's call, will always guide you toward your highest purpose. The less you think about it, the easier it is. Your mind is used to fantasising and conjuring loads of different obstacles. Remember to not get attached to any of them. Keep feeling, tuning in and listening. Keep exploring your inner realm. Keep owning whatever you find there, without apologising, or labelling the experience. The work is diligent and ongoing but so worth it!

If you think you are not the diligent type, take a second to look at your life so far. You have been diligent in your old patterns for years. You have defended, resisted, blamed, and attacked with the best of them. You have held on, made due, sacrificed. Be proud of the diligence that has gotten you to this point. Now, take that persistence and apply it directly to your re-patterning. Toss the junk out and bring in all the love waiting to help support you on this awesome journey of yours.

Naturally, you will usher people into the same kind of work you are doing whether via a course like "The Fearless Life Guide" or intuitively through other means. Keep in mind that every single path is valid, every single person's aliveness is valid. How could you ever think that one way is better or worse than another? Be open to possibilities. Assume everyone is trying to do their best, and send them your love.

Keep working within yourself to reach those higher vibrational states of loving awareness. You have to keep dissolving your arrogance. You have to keep dissolving the judgments when they arise.

Do not expect your wants to fit into your timeline right away. The old patterned thoughts will be happy to take you on a little ride. "I am doing the work, why isn't anything changing yet!? Why isn't everything exactly how I want it to be!?!"

Why does this happen? You are still attached and thinking the world is happening to you. You still think the bank needs to stop being so greedy. No. You have to stop being greedy. That is right, there is junk weighing you down. In the case of the bank, become over-flowingly generous. That is the best and only counter.

Know that you can walk away if it all gets too much. Watch Netflix, or YouTube. Turn off your inner work and numb out. Go play, and have fun! Enjoy the fruits of your inner labour unapologetically. Heck, go on holiday! You can come away from the work, and re-engage at any point. Just remain aware.

When you step away, things may appear different to you. If you decide to go back to watching TV, be really aware of how it makes you feel. Maybe you feel bombarded by the advertising or, cannot find any content that feels good to watch. Stay present always, no matter what you are doing.

The work you are doing is building momentum in your energy. Ride that wave and as you do, trust you will become greater aligned. Stay where it feels good, stay in the flow. When you hit a perceived rock, or obstacle of any kind, shift it, move it, or dissolve it and keep moving. Who knows where the limit is, if there is one at all? We might just burst through a shield and find ourselves in a completely different realm. Either way, it is all up to you. As a piece of star stuff, a light being, what are you going to vibrate while here?

In the end, diligence, schmiligence. Your commitment to the broader expansion is already sealed, because you are here.

Together, we are redefining love as service. Being a human, vibrating love, is the only work that you are here to do. Like any new skill, you become better and better with practice until eventually it becomes the natural way of things. Imagine entire communities practicing and living with an intention to love. You have started and will help lead the way.

Until then, throw a party! Invite all your friends. Ask them to meditate with you in the morning. Will they be up for the challenge?

9.3 Integrity

"Integrity is choosing your thoughts and actions based on values rather than personal gain." Anon

Integrity is about honesty, but in order to be truly honest, you have to know who you are. You have to be able to feel what resonates with you, which is of course, listening to your intuition.

With regards to the state of the world, honesty is struggling. Humans are in conflict with themselves; there is mass denial and resistance on a global scale. In this state, humanity remains bound to the illusions of fear and separation, unable to find honesty. They are afraid of themselves, and remain unwilling to feel any emotions that might ask them to choose differently. As a result, they perpetuate a state of mass dishonesty.

Once you become a self-responsible human being, your integrity is an important key. You know what the best thing is to do. Do that.

When you embody integrity, you are willing to "lose it all" to stay true to you. You know almost intuitively that nothing is actually owned, anyway. Let's be honest. We all live here and so, we all deserve to be here. Beyond class division, and the illusion of a corrupt power structure, every human being has a right to the basic necessities.

By taking responsibility for your life, you become responsible for the whole. By owning your guilt, you are no longer denying it, and can move to action. Your integrity will steer you in a direction that feels best. Standing firm in your integrity, you will do what is right, not what is comfortable. Once you break through the initial feelings of discomfort, when you are truly willing to let go of everything you fear to lose, you can harness the star power within, and shine.

Integrity will not let you live in fear. It will not let you hide from your truth. If you deny, or hide, you perpetuate the past, and your dream life will continue to elude you. Do not let it slip away, not now that you have come this far.

****

This process is scary. I know first-hand. There were times I thought I was crazy, that I should just try to fit in with everyone else, deny what I felt, follow the rules and pretend everything was okay. I wouldn't be alive to tell this tale of freedom if I had. I kept believing there was something better and that belief saved my life. I could not bear to deny the love and compassion I felt for humanity, so I dove into my guilt, shame, and pain and asked to hear Truth. I listened and heard the message: You can rise above the fear. And, that is exactly what I have done. Now, I live to share that message. My paradise is yours, too.

Being among the walking dead, or the storm troopers of our time, is not for me. If you have read to this point, I do not think it is for you, either. I broke down, and broke through, over and over again, and now, I am free. I chose to rise above all of the illusion and believe the world is a paradise where I can give unconditional love to everyone I meet. A place where I can learn lessons, and share what I know to be true. This, my friends, is freedom.

****

Your integrity's desire that you do what is right for you is freedom; no matter the consequences, no matter what you think you might lose. Allow the change. Paradise awaits you on the other side. I am with you all the way.

BONUS LESSON
Serious Not Sombre

Serious work does not have to be heavy and it most definitely should not feel sombre. This work is awesome. You are a transformer of dense emotions and old patterns. Although there are moments when you will feel heavy or serious, you are transforming yourself and detaching from the story of your heavy burdens. You are, in fact, freeing yourself of rigid seriousness, so the work, eventually becomes easier, not to mention, fun.

This is massive work that you are doing, and of course, if you are serious about living fearlessly, and serious about making radical changes in the world around you, then this is legitimately serious work you are doing. However, that is the flip, or the paradox as it were. The most serious work you will ever undertake is light, joyful, and ultimately fulfilling. The seriousness I am referring to is more about your being seriously committed to increasing your own levels of joy, to being seriously committed to feeling fulfilled and free, and to being seriously committed to loving as many people as possible through the light of your own compassion. If your seriousness becomes heavy and dogmatic and austere, you have lost the plot. You are in that case actually creating more barriers, more sombre, dense patterns within. Do not let that happen.

The ways in which you will really begin to change relate directly to how you use language and communicate with your entire feeling body. As we change, so does the structure of how we relate to, and communicate through, words. This includes the word serious. Seriously. I write about this because you may at times feel misunderstood due to your frequency jumps.

There is already a lot of miscommunication. We all experience it. You, however, are learning to become present and aware, attending to the other, listening without reacting. In this state, you can flow with your own good feelings rather than pushing against your external world. You can use you own awareness to disengage and actually avoid the drama altogether.

In every moment you can choose to see from a love-light perspective, or a contracted, limited one. Most people have just forgotten that they have a choice. This is part of your expanded responsibility; making choices. Remember, too, you can love people no matter what they choose. You can always choose to love another, and accept that if their awareness is only vibrating at a certain frequency, it may be that some distance is required to uplift your own. Again, it is about letting go and being aware of your own practice. Attune to your integrity, your self-responsibility, and detach from the energetic frequencies that no longer serve you.

This practice has great power to assist others even if at first glance it appears to upset them. In your imagination always practice lifting others up. If there is any pain in miscommunication, offer (if only in your mind and heart) sincere forgiveness to yourself, the other, and then extend love and light to the entire situation. You have a much greater impact on the entire collective when you are lightening up. Your job is to look for positive insight while enjoying yourself.

Living fearlessly is about finding your way to a more fluid way of life, one that for most of us living on the planet today, feels different. In the early stages, when you are unlocking all those chains so you can break out of the old ways, you might go through phases where you think the work is too hard, and super serious. Do not get stuck there, thinking it is serious. Instead, keep telling yourself this work wants you to laugh a whole lot at yourself, and at life. Because it really is not serious; it is a ride.

Eventually, with your new foundation firmly in place, life will feel easy.

Always keep in mind that you are consciousness; you are creation. You naturally dissolve triggers, and you flow through life in love with it all. You allow people to come and go, honouring their free will. You easily release judgments because you know they are only blocks to your bliss. You are no longer attached to anything because you trust that your life is unfolding perfectly. You have faith because you feel at one with your own heart, and can feel the difference between separation and oneness.

If there has to be any seriousness, it is more to do with the seriousness of your commitment to living fearlessly.

This work is not for everyone, but if you have made it this far, it is for you. Still, be willing to let this go at some point. You will know when you are ready to simply live in love and freedom, to let go of a process and to just live in joy. That is how freeing this guide is intended to be.

My vision is that one day there will be no need for courses, or healers. The world will be healed. You are here to find and define your vision. In the meantime, have fun on this awesome ride.

9.4 Star Power

So, what is your star power? Your star power is you living your highest purpose. And, it does not look like anything, but it feels like how it sounds, 'star' and 'powerful'.

Star power listens to the subtleties of your intuition and trusts it fully. Your star power is you loving the world with its conditions, and still seeing it moved beyond the conditions, beyond words, and beyond thought into an Eden. Your star power is a gentle, nurturing recognition of your aliveness. It affirms your inherent birth right to be joyful. This power breaks you down and rebuilds you with a stronger foundation.

Your star power is a sacred recognition of the oneness of life. In your divine state you can step back, hold your arms wide open and embrace all the pain, all the violence, and the fearful illusions of separation. The power you have when aligned to your highest self is limitless and does not ask how many crystals you have, how long you can sit in meditation, how fit your body is, how many courses you have done, or how much money you have.

Your star power holds the memory of your heart song; the melody given you in the beginning. It is your birth right. When aligned with your star power you feel totally blessed, totally abundant, and totally looked after. This is where trust lives, where you find faith in your darkest moments. Star power is the deepest part of your silence, and the beauty and simplicity of your presence. Star power knows when to say no, and when to say, yes. It knows when to say, I am sorry.

Star power knows how and when to rise, and when to speak your truth. Star power will guide you each step of the way.

And it is not just for you, it is for everybody. How you show up in life matters. Your presence reminds people that they have a voice, too. That they are powerful, too. That they do not need to stay silent in the face of injustice, in the face of poverty and lack. That they can stand up and connect and rise from within their own divine sacred connection in truth, knowing that there is infinite abundance, enough for all. You lead them out of the darkness and into the light, through your own presence. It is not through your words. Not necessarily through your actions, either. Just by being you, vibrating the essence of your own truth. Your very presence will wake up their own cellular memory. Something will be sparked just by seeing you. Just by being near you. A remembrance of their own star power.

Star power is showing up with all your scars, and wounds, and choosing to keep showing up. It never ends, your divinity knows that. You are no longer here to apologise for speaking too loudly, for being too beautiful, or for not having the right dress size. No longer are you going to apologise for having the strength you have, or for being in a state of loving compassion. No apologising for being joyful and vibrant, for being the mothers, fathers, sons and daughters that we are.

No longer are you going to silence that part of you. No longer are you going to remain disconnected out of fear of your own greatness. You are going to shine. You are going to find that little girl or boy who once cried at all the violence on TV and give them a big loving hug. Let them cry as much as needed until you can feel they are free, safe to play and enjoy life.

You and the child you once were are shining. Keep going. Keep loving.

9.5 Authenticity

"Authenticity is freedom from the illusion of fear and alignment to the reality of love." George Lizos

Authenticity requires you to be real, genuine, and vulnerable. If authentic, you know what integrity means. Everyone is authentic at heart, but many do not know how to access their authenticity having been taught uniformity. They have hidden who they are because they believe being a slave to a system of control and domination is all they can hope for. They think being miserable and mediocre is normal and that shiny people are nuisances or "special".

You are breaking free from those misconceptions, making a conscious decision to become free. Miserable is not in your vocabulary now, and you are choosing to shine no matter what anyone thinks. You are reengaging with your authentic self. Authenticity is simply your unique essence expressing itself fully. Nothing more; nothing less.

You needn't try to be authentic, it is there under the layers of masks you made when trying to be someone you were not. The masks are energy, of course, and do not solely belong to you. They belong to the entire collective, which is why you are doing this work; to dissolve energetic density passed down by your ancestors, by all of our ancestors.

Deoxyribonucleic acid, or DNA, is present in nearly all living matter. It is the carrier of genetic information. It is generally understood that we carry cellular imprints from the past in our DNA. Certainly most religious traditions espouse this belief, so hopefully it is helpful to learn that emotional storms are not just about you in this lifetime, but linked with the emotions of your parents, grandparents, and so on. This is what I am referring to when I speak of "karmic backlog". You are clearing who knows how many decades of emotional wounds.

Those who do not resonate with this work, have other work to do. That is why it is important to honour free will, and respect one another's choices. Everyone has a unique purpose and message in the awakening of humanity. There is no one left behind even though during this transition phase it may appear to be so.

When viewing life and humanity from a perspective of oneness, it is impossible to fathom anyone ever being left behind. This life is a game of our choosing, a matrix of our own imagination, and a journey of our soul's ever expanding desires. We all chose this. The more you can own your choosing and take responsibility for your life, the better it gets. The more you deny, the more fearful and toxic it gets. Funnily, your "toxic" can be someone else's pleasure, which is why we must learn to release our judgments, and simply let people be. To transform your illusions is the only responsibility you bear.

Tell yourself to go ahead and be wonderfully, radiantly, authentically you.

9.6 Vitality: *The Force*

Vitality is the essence of your life force. It is in everything you do. It is in each breath you take. Igniting your vitality for life is about owning and recognising your various roles and responsibilities in creating the ongoing manifestation of your life. Enslavement is the opposite of this, which means a slow and painful death; a sickly, disempowered life. The more vital you are, the more alive and creative you are. If you feel tired, you rest. If you want something you go get it.

As mentioned previously, each of us has our own unique heart song, or signature frequency. The work of pulling back the veils, facing the shadows and dismantling blocks can be exhausting, but in the aftermath, energy is restored. You feel up-lifted and find your vitality increased. It is as if you have come alive, attuned now to your own vital essence.

You can increase your vitality by doing the steps herein and continuing to choose freedom from old and destructive pat-terns. Dealing with yourself honestly is a massive undertaking, but you wouldn't be reading this guidebook if you weren't capa-ble of it. You are strong enough to sit with the pain, turmoil, heartache, terror, and loss, and fearlessly love it all. In the act of seeing it, feeling it and loving it, you begin to transform it, dis-solve it, and set yourself free.

You are strong. You are vital. You are capable. Do not ever let anyone convince you otherwise. You are powerful, guided by an ageless intuition that knows exactly what is best for you. Take a moment and listen. Can you hear your heart song humming? That is you, you know, humming a joyful tune. Now, can you feel it? Ah, vitality restored and pulsing through your veins.

To step up your vitality, incorporate these little practices into your daily life:

✓ Go outside in the morning, open your arms wide, take a deep breath, and say meaningfully, "Thank you. I love my life".

✓ Find enjoyable ways of slowing down and taking care of yourself. This may include lighting incense when taking a bath. Do anything that expands your relaxation practice. Deep rest is essential to increasing your vitality.

- ✓ Luxuriously embrace your moments of self-care and rest.
- ✓ Spend at least a couple of minutes every day breathing as deeply and as slowly as you can. Be mindful.
- ✓ Have fun moving around. Put music on. Dance. Stretch. Run. Play. Let your movement practice fit your mood. But do move every day.
- ✓ Love your body. Give yourself a hug. Caress your skin (even if it feels uncomfortable, or odd, do it anyway).
- ✓ Love your food. Be thankful for every single bite.
- ✓ Pamper yourself and make plans for things that excite the hell out of you.

There is no time limit on these activities. Even adding a minute here and a minute there into your daily life will have a huge impact. Free yourself to go ahead and embrace your vitality, embrace your aliveness, and savour it. Keep working in tandem with triggers, with your guilt, or whatever comes up for you. Practice loving it all.

Fill yourself up with the excitement of how wonderful this world is. Feel it in your heart. Now, imagine it even better and remind yourself that you are here to change things because you want to change. And, you are.

Keep going.

9.7 What To Expect

Expect to be releasing some your biggest challenges now, or at least becoming very aware of, and more comfortable with, facing them. Expect to be feeling more deeply aware of and empowered in your intuitive abilities, innate gifts, and newly uncovered talents.

Whatever your big challenges are, whether relationship stuff, money worries, or body image issues, trust that as you own them fully, and transform your emotional triggers to them, your physical patterns will miraculously change. Do not rush this, though. Address each thing in your own time. And, keep in mind, encouragement is found in the little things.

Are you appreciating your body more? Have you noticed more feelings of gratefulness? Are you worrying less? Has money started showing up in new and unexpected ways? Have you found yourself drawn to a new activity, or group of people?

The most important thing is that you are noticing it all, becoming more aware. No matter how painful, or miserable you feel in moments, as long as you accept that the feeling is there, and patiently watch it do its thing, it will pass.

Give yourself a big pat on the back, better yet, a round of applause. Not just for reading this book, or for losing weight, or making more money, but for showing up to do this work. You are an explorer, an adventurer, no longer going along with the status quo, but breaking free from the status quo to come alive! You are breaking free from misery and mediocrity and encouraging others to do the same. You are making the world a happier place, by choosing to be happy. Is that not the coolest?

You are breaking through all your fears and judgments. You are reclaiming your divinity, true abundance, and radiant beauty. And, you are choosing to see that same divinity in all you encounter. You are beginning to see your perfection and know that everyone else is perfect, too.

Perfection knows there are actually no mistakes. Those things we call mistakes are merely more experiences meant to teach, or expand us. "Mistakes" catapult us into a new phase, a next level of awareness. And, because we all have a unique way of growing and learning, we make different "mistakes". After all, we are all here for different reasons, so, if you are comparing, thinking, "Oh, no! They have moved along to the next step before me. They must be smarter than I am!" or, "She has loads of money. She must be way better at the Law of Attraction" you would be off base. No one is ever better or worse than anyone else.

Thoughts like these hang around when your emotions are triggered. For example; you still feel jealous when the girl sitting next to you gets attention from a boy you like, or you still feel like a victim when you get bank charges. These triggers are telling you that you are still vibrating on a certain level, which means your thought frequency will also be at that level. See it clearly for what it is, feel the separation, then begin to transform it. See yourself as one with the other. Feel into the unity. All ways.

You are feeling more secure and grounded in your integrity now, so when you notice yourself slipping off, it should be easier to get back. You are starting to see the fruits of your labour, working on the inside and shape-shifting in your external world.

Be sure to tell yourself, you are doing this, creating this. You are making this choice so you deserve the reward, you deserve the applause. You have stepped up to take responsibility. Own your power, and do the work. You deserve every joy you can think of.

Step 9. Take Responsibility & Claim Your Star Power

Exercise A.

Where are you still blaming, complaining, attacking or making excuses? Be specific. Write it down. Be prepared to discuss.

Exercise B.

With journal to hand, silently ask yourself these 5 questions and write down the answers you receive. Be prepared to share and discuss.

1. Why are you doing what you're doing?
2. What makes you excited?
3. What makes you feel passion?
4. What is your ultimate vision for your life?
5. What challenges do you face?

Exercise C.

You're taking responsibility, well done! You are starting to feel pretty awesome and powerful. You are looking good. You're feeling really on top of this material and things are generally feeling sweet. It almost feels like you're done. You've arrived. You are already there. And then one day, you're sitting at a coffee shop and someone walks past you and you notice yourself pass a sly judgment, "If she wasn't drinking Coca-Cola, she'd probably be thinner." Busted!

Brutal. The distorted mind is super sneaky! Pay attention in those moments. As soon as you've spotted a judgment, look at it, own it, harmonise it (by sending that person you just judged some lovin') and enlighten it. Apply the bandage of forgiveness and move on.

After reading the above, can you recall slipping into judgment in the last 24 hours? If so, make a note of it and be prepared to share.

Exercise D.

Did you meet with any resistance, judgments or triggers while absorbing the material in this Step? If so, write down the specifics of your experience.

Exercise E.

Tap into your star power. Can you recall a time when you wanted to speak up and you didn't? How did it feel? Describe the experience. Be prepared to share.

Exercise F.

Over the weeks have you noticed anything that you might consider to be more karmic in nature? Describe your experience and be willing to share and discuss.

Step 10. Living Imagination

10.1 Imagination

Imagination is your infinite creative potential. And you have access to it always. When children most of us live in our imaginations, until, told repeatedly to "get real" and stop day-dreaming, we then tune out of our inner world, and tune in to the outer. Your job now, is to reawaken your imagination and re-member how to have fun with it so you can start having fun in the "real world", which is, the world through your eyes, a world that desperately needs you to tap back into your imagination.

It is helpful to be reminded that much of our external real-ity was once in someone's imagination. We did not always have cars, or airplanes, for example. Only birds could fly, right? It seems laughable now, of course, but once, not so. Visionaries (just like you) challenged convention and imagined more. Leo-nardo Da Vinci's aircraft might have had its limitations, but be-cause of his (and others, of course) imagination, humans can fly now.

When you spend more time imagining, you expand as-pects of your consciousness by seeing potential that might not have previously existed (for you). Remember, separation is an il-lusion. Nothing you perceive outside of you is separate from you, from the consciousness that is you. Recognise that everything you are perceiving has already been created and agreed upon by the collective consciousness.

236

Your imagination gets muddled with the conditions, and restrictions in place externally. You think limitations and obstacles are real and imagination is a waste of time, hence deeply entrenched emotional reactive patterns push against creativity and you perpetuate painful patterns.

Awakening means you are waking up. No more nightmares with you as the victim "out there". Once awakened, you are clear that you are the only creator in your reality and have the ability to see where your energy is tangled up in thoughts, or energies that do not resonate with you and what you are capable of creating. Once you embody this on a cellular level, you are limitless, and the world, your world, really is in the palm of your hands, or more accurately, in the frequency emission of your true hearts desires.

To see your imagination come to life, there must be a foundational shift in how you relate to your own mind/body/spirit. It is one system. Calling aspects conscious or subconscious, ego or imagination, does not mean they are separate in any way. On the contrary, it simply shows how magnificently powerful you are. These components are part of your oneness, ushering you toward greater expansion if you choose to work with them.

****

The global awakening is happening as more and more minds remember their own creative potential and use it for expansion, compassion, and love. You will continue to be triggered if you are still out for personal gain, or are holding false perceptions. The awakening is happening whether you like or not; whether we are ready for it or not. So, own your junk, lift the lid on your denial and prepare for sweeping positive change.

It really is all in your mind. You are either being enslaved by your own mind telling you there are just too many limitations, barriers, and walls, or you are telling yourself you are free to make your own decisions. Right now, following along with this guide, you are unlocking, unravelling and transforming thoughts and patterns, not for yourself alone, but for your ancestors and the entire collective. You have already agreed to do it for them, by the way. That is why you were born into the privileged few. Those born of privilege are responsible for those born of lack. We must imagine them in abundance and safety, and ourselves free from any destructive material chains - stuff we buy into that doesn't serve the collective any more. We owe it to ourselves.

****

The power of your imagination is your creative connection to infinite possibilities. You just have to believe in it. Believe that you are here to create the life you wish to experience. When you do, you dissolve a neediness for things outside of you and you begin working solely on your own energetic frequency as a means of imagining and then creating that experience which you desire for your own soul's expansion.

As you continue to transform old patterns and thoughts into new and lighter ones, notice how your imagination comes to life. What you begin to sense, and see with your awareness, is more of your multidimensional makeup and your intrinsic connection to all life, and your imagination is reignited. It is exciting to paint a broader view of reality, rather than the mechanical, limited world view that we have all been bumbling along in for so long.

This is the merging. You are merging with your imagination, and coming to live fully in a space of deep trust and positive expectation all the time.

EXERCISE: Imagine you are on the edge of a cliff and you feel free. Your arms are wide open and you are exuding love for all life. You feel fearless. Now, step off the edge of the cliff. Are you going to let yourself fall, or do you trust that the moment you put your foot down, a step will appear? Feel your bravery, see yourself taking that step no matter how scared you are. Just do it. Keep moving forward. Each step is getting easier because you know the next step will appear. You do not need to rush. There is no need to panic. The next step is always there.

This is where you want to be living - on the edge. Not like an adrenaline junkie seeking the next thrill, but in a state of fearlessness when it comes to facing your life, which in this context, is about you facing all of your limitations. You are unlimited, start living it.

You are making manifest a world where people play, celebrate and create from Love. Keep playing, and keep merging with your imagination because it is you.

And remember: You are awesome.

10.2 Vision

"Make your vision so clear that your fears become irrelevant."
Anonymous

From the system's perspective, vision is simply seeing with your eyes. Having a "vision" is often considered otherworldly, weird, and not a reliable or consistent way of seeing; like seeing ghosts or having drug-induced hallucinations. The latter experiences are deemed delusions. Anything unseen is therefore unbelievable, not to be trusted. We know better now.

****

"The Fearless Life Guide" was born out of a little girl's dream. The horror, violence, and poverty I saw was heart-breaking. Kids made fun of me because I cried so much when watching movies, and when I could not be mean to the different kids at school, I suffered more ridicule. But, I have always been sensitive and compassionate, despite layers of distortions and my own efforts to deny it, my compassionate heart remained intact.

240

At one time, I wanted to become a doctor in order to save lives. Eventually I had to admit that sciences were not my strong subjects, and so, decided to become a famous actress. I would be of value in the world's eyes then, and could share all my money with those in need. People would listen as I spoke my truth. This pursuit nearly killed me so, I decided to be me.

By this time, I'd had enough of the world. I did not want to play "its" games anymore. The way I felt, I had no other choice. I simply wanted to live in peace. So, I began to accept my weird-ness by taking responsibility for my life. I forgave everyone, my-self included, and started to honour the little girl's dream of a peaceful and joyful world.

With the help of my committed yoga practice, and daily journaling, I started letting go of all that I had learned and began transforming a whole lot of guilt, pain, and shame. I dove in and owned it all keeping my vision firmly in place all the while.

People started to show up for me. Teachers, healers, and plenty of weirdos who felt the same way; that all you need is Love. My new support system started to rebuild, and the vision of the world I wanted to live in began to manifest.

No one else's ideas mattered to me, not if they didn't feel good. No opinions, judgments, or assumptions triggered me any longer. I was arriving home, coming into the light of my own es-sential and divine self.

Today, I want for nothing, and am more abundant than I have ever been in every sense of the word. I need only continue to hold the vision and do the work. This is my gift to the world. I am so grateful to honour the little girl I had almost forsaken.

****

Vision and imagination are great friends. You have the power to imagine anything. And yet, not one of us has the exact same imaginative vision, because we all have unique gifts and talents to share. Vision relates to your most epic dreams and divine life purpose. Vision feels different than the broader imaginative mental capacity. It will feel more specific and more real to you. Your intuition will help you decipher what your specific vision is, as will your life experiences. As long as you continue to choose to feel good, relaxed, and joyful, you are on the right track.

Once the clouds of judgment, resistance, and denial clear, your ability to enjoy playing with your imagination will most definitely expand. Let it. Begin to imagine your dream life, and all that will happen there. When you have a charged vision, you may begin to quiver, or you could say, vibrate, intensely. You might experience goose bumps or a shiver up your spine. These are signs that the specific vision you are forming has something to do with your divine purpose; it is meant for you, otherwise you would not be able to feel it so tangibly.

As you expand and raise your frequency and integrate your higher vibrations by becoming responsible and grounded, the ongoing embodiment process will further crystallise your awakening and accelerate your transformation. Now that you are thinking of yourself as light energy frequency, begin to dialogue with this part of you. Ask for more insight, more clarity, and expect to receive intuitive guidance, or to have experiences that offer you what you are asking for. Again, you are creating it all, but it is sort of like a puzzle. Be patient. There is always a bit of unlearning in every process as you learn a new way of being.

As you continue to accept that your imagination is a truly divine gift, your visions will become clearer. Are you imagining heart-based models for living? Do you see sustainable eco villages which are harmonious, luxurious, celebratory, sacred, and super high vibing places? Have faith in your vision. We have the ability to create a world where everyone is free to live their potential, where everyone is safe, has space, shelter, food and access to learning within a supportive and loving community. Hold the vision and start creating that world in your life.

Creation is infinite. Imagine a world where everyone is loved and cared for. Imagine a peaceful, infinitely abundant and harmonious world. Feel it. Hold true to your vision no matter what other people think or say, no matter how deluded they think you are.

Humanity has the capacity to create harmony, too.

"Create the highest, grandest vision possible for your life, because you become what you believe." Oprah

Keep going. Your vision is creating your world. Work it, save yourself the hard labour so that you can playfully create a new world from the highest, most awesome vision you can conjure.

10.3 Create New Things

Now that you are uplifting yourself, and consciously aware of intending your vibration to be one of love and unity, you will gain access to an expansive landscape of innovative ideas, and inspiration. Allow yourself to think bigger, and be willing to create from this place.

What do you really want? Maybe six months ago, or two years ago, you had a particular dream you shrugged off because you thought you could never have it, or make it happen. Well now, you know you can. Rearrange your mind so that you can have it all. Remind yourself that you can be that happy! Look lovingly at your fears and see them for what they are, then choose something better. Choose something bigger. Choose something awesome!

When you were little, you used to play and hang out in your imagination all the time. You were constantly conjuring up more ways to play and have fun. Along the way, on your journey into adulthood, the child-like innocence, playfulness, and big imagination got squashed. Now, however, you can revisit that time of innocence and dive back into your playfulness and imagination.

How can you enlighten others? What steps are you being guided to take? How can you inspire others to make the shift? Well, it should not feel like hard work, it should feel inspired. The only fear you will face comes from breaking out of your own comfort zone. You know already, however, that you need to do this in order to be free.

One helpful hint is to organise local get-togethers. Throw a party, even a festival, whatever inspires you. Set up workshops to share your affirmations and meditation techniques with people. Let people in on what you are doing. You may not know it yet, but people want to know. They might not know it yet, but somewhere deep within they are curious about all this "spiritual" stuff. If they are not feeling good about life, then there will be a part of them intrigued by the idea of transformation. You can help.

Keep asking yourself, "How can I be of service? How can I contribute more?" Follow through with the action steps you are guided to take. Your intuition wants what is best for you so listen to it. You continue to help others by raising yourself up, by raising the bar and living a joyful and abundant life. In this rising, you are helping to dissolve greed, corruption, and separation, while at the same time, strengthening Love. Keep going. Keep creating from this place.

How fearlessly can you live? You have so many beautiful dreams. There are places in the world you want to visit, communities you want to support. Call on your visions and commit to them with every fibre of your being. Commit to the highest vision that you have for yourself and for all of humanity.

10.4 Expectation

"The greatest gift you can give someone is your highest expectation of them." Esther "Abraham" Hicks

Expectation is a feeling you have with regards to an upcoming event or situation. It also relates strongly to how you regard life in general as in, do you expect good things to happen to you, or not? Your dominant vibration, whether worrisome or fearless, is an expectant output and therefore, your creative force field.

If you are worried, complaining, or anxious about anything at all, you are in a negative vibrational state, which means you are expecting a negative outcome. You will most likely realise that outcome. If, however, you are excited, relaxed, and grateful about something, you are in a state of positive expectation and cool things are going to happen.

Be aware that your mind can always rationalise yourself out of something, but feelings do not lie. You can tell yourself you are excited about something, but if you are not, you are not. We lie to ourselves, a lot. For this work to succeed, an absolute commitment to brutal honesty is required.

****

The distorted-mind-world, is typically geared toward negative expectations, and that attitude perpetuates itself breeding apathy and complacency. "Why bother at all? Nothing will turn out right."

On the flip side, there exists the "everything is perfect" view. These polarised views keep us quite numb as we go about our days expecting someone to rescue us from debt, or our unfulfilling jobs. At least, we assure ourselves, we are better off than the poor sods on this planet who have no food and are being bombed out of their homes. Well, it is time to wake up.

****

Positive expectation is not about getting attached to any specific outcome, no matter how clear your vision is. Expectation is only ever about how you feel NOW. Any attachment to how you think things should be will only loop you back into patterns of control wherein you believe you know exactly what you deserve, and when everything should fall into place.

Positive expectation is light-hearted. What you expect is that all is well, so all will be well. You expect an outcome that is best for you, always. If surprised, disappointed, or saddened, by an outcome, return to a place of gratitude reminding yourself that you expect only what is in your highest purpose always.

In order to expect positive change, more of us must stop moaning about everybody else, and start expecting new things to show up. Start to expect things to go your way. Expect your dreams to become reality; in a grounded and loving way, because you deserve it, and so does everyone else. Expect to behave differently and make different choices. As your vibration changes, so too will your actions and therefore your outcomes.

You did not come here to be a slave to negative expectations. It does not feel good to feel that everything is lousy and will continue that way. You came here to learn, and to feel what it is like to be human. You came here to feel the fullness of life, and the richness of this planet in its varied and exquisite form. Expect that. Expect to feel more love, more awe, and more richness in your connections to others and this planet. Expect to live in your integrity, no matter how uncomfortable it feels, or makes others feel. Expect to share your creativity with all you meet. Expect to be overflowing with joy when you see others fulfilling their dreams. Expect life to unfold miraculously, as you let go of trying to control every little detail. Control is not up to you, how you vibrate and manage your energy is.

Start to get excited about life again. Start to get juiced up about how much fun you are going to have and how many beautiful souls you are going to meet along the way. Now that you have remembered who you truly are, have been shaken up by the depth and power of your emotional body and come to know that your body is not to be feared, you can get excited. You are a vessel of pure potential designed and made specifically by you.

Do you want to choose to love and live fearlessly? Or, live and love in fear. Exactly. The choice is a no-brainer.

Start to expect awesome. When some fear comes up, you know how to handle it; breathe through it and laugh in its face because, you know that is not who you want to be anymore.

Living in a state of positive expectation occurs almost naturally when enough of the old patterns and dense energies have transformed to let you live like a child again, innocent and free. Of course, you are a mature and conscious adult. You have just decided to reclaim your innocence.

Remind yourself that you are establishing new foundational pillars for a new life. Your new core values are being established as you continue to change, breakthrough, and choose to live your highest purpose, fearlessly. Trust that more and more minds are doing the same. You are supporting the momentum. Keep going.

BONUS LESSON
Affirmation and Mantra

Affirmations are positive thoughts or short sentences and work wonders when you really feel and embody the meaning, or vibrational essence of the words.

Mantras are the language equivalent of yoga, usually repeated a lot, they vibrate on a positive frequency, invoking positive vibrational results within you. Mantras are often sung and are really good fun when you can just let go and sing from your heart. You do not have to have a "good voice" to sing.

Singing is a great way to release emotion and to raise your vibes. The reason I say this, is because, as a once aspiring performer, because I did not have a great singing voice, I shut down and stopped singing completely. As I began to step into my power, singing was something I began to do again, whether in the shower, a singing lesson, or driving in the car, and boy-o-boy is it liberating! Once you can get over your conditioning about whether you sing well or not, just let it rip. You will feel an instantaneous lift. Like movement, deep breathing and silence, singing is right up there with ways to bring on those feel good vibes.

Affirmations are a really great way to assist you in reprogramming your mind to be more harmonious. Simply put, if you pay attention and connect to the words, you will find combinations that feel good to you, that calm you down, lighten you up, or inspire you and so on. Affirmations and mantras actually hold a certain vibration. Depending on the sound frequency and how well you connect to it determines how much of that vibrational essence you invoke.

At this stage, use all of the tools you have access to. You can use affirmations as a way to clear density when you are sitting with a lot of emotional discomfort. You can use mantra on a regular basis if it soothes you, or helps you feel more grounded. The important thing, as you already know, is that it feels good and you are speaking or thinking words from your heart.

An affirmation could be simply "I am love-light", or "I am radiant love". However, if you are only mechanically repeating the words and not embodying them, they are not being absorbed. This means they are having little to no effect on your vibration. In this case, it may be that more shifts need to take place in order to reconnect the mind and body.

Play around. Get creative and make up affirmations relevant to your themes and challenges. If money tugs at you, create a money affirmation that dissolves your worry, like, "I am infinitely abundant" or "I am totally supported and everything I need always shows up in perfect timing" or, this is one a friend came up with, "I always have more than enough".

Affirmations can bring you into a more connected place, one aligned with your unique and creative inner voice. Know that you have your own unique way of connecting, and that these are just some tips and tools to help you live fearlessly.

10.5 Crystallising

Crystallising is to make something definite or concrete. As you continue to transform, your new patterns will take definite form. Also, by this point, if you have been doing the work and exercises with diligence, you have heightened your vibrations. You are simply more aware, and more attuned at a different level. That frequency will begin to crystallise for you with continued use and ongoing practice.

At some point along your journey, your vision of yourself will also begin to crystallise. You cannot force this, it will happen naturally as you begin to embody more light and accelerate in your transformational process and thus, hold greater mental clarity with regards to living your vibrational reality.

Once you get to the stage of crystallisation, you will already be well aware of momentum and acceleration in your life. You will have had some profound emotional experiences, or breakthroughs, and recognise the increase in your vibrational frequency. Things might have started to get freaky for you, but you are loving it all because you have basically bottomed out with all your fears and are becoming fearless.

As a fearless being, your experience in, and relationship with the world, is vastly different from the way it was. Things that used to bother you no longer do because you know what is going on in a more profound and uniquely you way. "Out there" is not scary to you anymore. You know full well, you have come a long way, baby!

You are comfortable in your authenticity and because you always listen to your intuition, your life experiences continue to get better and better. Still, there are challenges and emotions and new themes that arise, but they are easier to handle. You have coping skills you did not have before.

Life no longer feels like a toxic burdensome wasteland. You see the beauty and plenty instead. You can laugh through the tears, the confusion, and the absolute weirdness of it all, re-lieved and grateful for the experiences you encounter. You con-tinue to learn with an open, loving heart.

Your ability to listen and respect your energy is improving and so, your vitality, well-being and ease also improves. It is to-tally awesome! Your encounters are more aligned and life just blows you away, repeatedly.

Your only practice now is to notice when you get sucked back into lower frequencies. When that happens, remain respon-sible for your own energy field. Remain committed to your vision, and hold the entire collective in the frequency of love, light, free-dom, and abundance. Nothing short of living a totally epic and miraculous life will do.

If any aspects are not yet fully crystallising, they won't feel locked in. You will feel as if those "things" are outside of you. You know the answers are within, so ask for what you need, es-pecially in meditation. Pose the question to your higher self. Also, review the lessons. Whatever decision you make, if you sincerely want to resolve any issue, the answer will present itself to you.

It is only ever your fear that could be holding someone, or something, away from you. Open your heart, break down the walls, and feel the light of your own love. Radiate it out as far as you can and crystallise your vision of an abundant and harmoni-ous new world. Stand tall and be proud of yourself. Let your light shine!

10.6 Living the Dream

Now, you have to muster the courage to actually live your dream. It may sound weird since you have spent your life thinking about it, working toward it, then forgetting it, only to wish for it and even fantasise about it. Now you are reading a book that is encouraging you to live it; and to continue to live it, because it never ends.

Once you accomplish satisfying one dream, there will be another and another and another. That is part of the illusion that points us to one dream, and one dream only, whether it be finding Prince Charming or landing the perfect job. It is all part of the same idea that once you get to a particular point that is it. Done.

Why we buy into that myth is a mystery. Lives do not unfold in one magical event. Far from it. They unfold in one magical event after another. Perhaps if we stood still long enough in the moment, we would realise that "there" is actually "here". Once you get "there" you have merely arrived at another "here". Neither life nor your desire to experience it suddenly stops.

When something happens that shakes up your entire world, starts you questioning and introduces you to a better feeling state, are you going to keep loving and working it? Or will you retract, and deny you ever broke through? Are you going to head back into your former role? Unlikely.

Living your dream requires fortitude, courage, and stamina, but ask anyone who does and they will straight up tell you it is worth it. Every. Time. So, if you are fed up with all the corruption you see, all the heartache, the unfairness, and poverty, face it and start to live your truth already.

Start being nice to people, or not, if you have no energy. You do not owe anyone anything. The only person you are responsible for is you. And you are only of service to your fellow humans when you become responsible, loving, and respectful to self. That is the paradox of modern life. We tend to think being of service looks like something; like Mother Teresa (although she was totally in service and an epic creator of beautiful dreams), but that is not the point. The point is, we copy one another, thinking that it looks like something which, of course, it does not. Mother Teresa was following her heart, listening to her intuition. She withstood because she believed in what she was doing with her whole being. If you being of service looks like that, you have nailed it. Otherwise, you are merely pretending, doing something that you think looks good and are not fully integrated in your fearlessness.

Our world needs more authenticity, more realness, and more people just being brutally honest about how they feel, and what they are going through. The world needs more people who are willing to quit jobs they hate, end abusive relationships, and quietly say a "positive no" to violence, bigotry, and slander, so we can come up with a better way. A way that allows and encourages creativity that takes care of one another. A way that upholds a higher standard for living for all. A way that nurtures and upholds Earth and all her inhabitants.

Somewhere we got lost and horribly confused. Now, as we awaken, we are beginning to remember our purpose, one mind at a time, enlightening more minds all at once.

It is okay if you do not want to live your dream. It is okay if it is too much, or too deep, or too weird. You can live however you want to live. This Guide is for those who are ready to take the leap and unapologetically live their truth no matter what it looks like, without judgment, from a loving and deeply compassionate heart.

10.7 What To Expect

Expect things to be a bit weird by now. If things are getting too weird for you, go back to the beginning, or leave it all behind. Do what feels best and most relevant to you. It is all okay. You are great, no matter what you choose.

By now you should be understanding that the more you trust your feel good flow, the quicker your transformation will be. The more you allow and relax, the quicker your new reality will begin to unfold in front of your eyes.

You know at this point, you should not be making this hard work. Sitting through emotional triggers, waves, and storms has become a new way of living, and you are no longer blaming the external world for how you feel. No more excuses. You know it is all about you and that you are one with everything and everyone else.

For the most part, you are enjoying your new way of relating to yourself, other people, and the world around you. You are feeling in love with life, and it is filling you up. You feel more magical and inspired; there is a twinkle in your eye and people stare at you a little longer than usual. It is the star shining out that they see, by the way.

You are beginning to embody, or crystallise, your belief that a new, improved life is not only attainable, but sustainable. The good life in not only found in movies or fairy tales. You know you are the creator in your world and so, you are choosing to create a world that gets better and better, all the time. You are choosing it to be so.

You are now fully aware that every time you sit through an emotional storm, you are rising up, and enlightening the entire collective. Along with feeling lighter emotionally, you are feeling more playful and innocent, and more in awe of the world around you. The world might appear more colourful and clear to you, and people may also look shinier.

On the occasions you find yourself away from your normal environment, say, at a wedding or on vacation, emotions might be kicked into high gear. Be aware of this possibility and know it is perfectly normal. You are changing your perception of the world around you at a core level, seeing with new eyes as it were, returning to a degree of innocence which makes the old, new again. If you find yourself suddenly unsteady, do not let an almost automatic surprise response throw you for too long. Recognise what is going on and allow your inner knowing to take charge. You are safe and there is nothing to fear. Keep breathing and ensure you are in touch with your intuition.

Stepping out of your day-to-day always opens you up. You have been altering routines and heightening awareness daily, walking away from the ordinary can cause a rush of feelings to surface. It is all good and perfectly okay, as mentioned, but realise it can bring up feelings of overwhelming insecurity, confusion, and profound sadness. Do what you have been doing. Allow, do not react, and know it will pass. Be grateful. Nothing is ever going to be the same. That is transformation!

Step 10. Living Imagination

Exercise A.

Imagine being on the edge of a cliff and you're super free. Your arms are wide open and you are in love with life. You are fearless. Now, step off the edge of the cliff. Are you going to let yourself fall or trust that the moment you put your foot down, a step will appear? Feel your bravery, see yourself taking that step no matter how scary it feels. Just do it. Stay on the edge and keep moving forward, each step getting easier with the knowing that the next step will appear. You don't need to rush, you do not need to panic. The next step will always show up.

What comes up for you when doing this exercise? Write it down and be prepared to share.

Exercise B.

What is the highest vision you hold for your life? Please describe and be prepared to share.

Exercise C.

Answer the following questions:

1. How can I be of service?
2. How can I contribute more?
3. What action steps are you being guided to take?

Note: your intuition only wants what's best for you and everyone else; listen to it, knowing you are coming from a place of Love and that your highest joy is for the greater good.

Exercise D.

Imagine a world where anything is possible, where you can be and do anything you want. You can be a superhero, a modern day Robin Hood if you want. You can do and be anything you desire, you just have to be responsible and use your intuition to stay in alignment with your star imagination and vision. Otherwise, the distorted mind will keep coming back in, to give you a slap whenever you buy into something that's not in unity with All That Is. Expect to keep learning.

Be prepared to share your "anything is possible" world.

Exercise E.

Where are you still being triggered? Dive deep and be as honest as possible. Be willing to share and discuss.

Exercise F.

Describe, in detail, what living your dream life feels like. Be prepared to share and discuss.

Step 11. Rest & Relaxation

11.1 Trust

"Always trust your gut. It knows what your head hasn't figured out yet." Anon

Trust. All of the material has been leading you to this. You either have it, or you do not. If you do not, you need to stop trying so hard, worrying so much, and trust the process. Let go already! Your worries are not serving you. Worry has never served anyone. It is a learned response which keeps us in a stress filled mess.

Trust is the opposite of worry, stress, and anxiety; it is the soother of those feelings. It carries you through the transformation process into liberation.

There is a part of you that remembers trust but purposely squashes any memory of it. Why? Growing up you noticed very little trust in action. People you loved made promises to you, then broke them. People told you lies. Doors were locked, fences made higher. You absorbed a great deal of fear energy, fear of a "system" out to get you, and that you had no power over. The media bombarded you with pictures of destruction, violence, and death. You came to fear the "other". Trust? No way! You have learned how foolish it is to trust. It is much better to stay closed off, wrapped up in your own little bubble. Is it?

Trust is real and has nothing to do with other people and everything to do with you. Furthermore, it is your ally in transformation. It is your best friend as you continue to become a fearless being. Always replace doubt with trust. It will support you in cultivating honest and healthy relationships in every area of your life.

Trust is relaxation. Trust is ease. Trust is allowing. Trust is basically the backbone of this whole book. If you can crystallise a state of trust, you are good to go. Job done. Trust is knowing guidance and support is always there for you. Again, replace doubt with trust in every scenario. Doubt supports lack, anxiety, and worry. We solidify doubt into our lives when we choose to own someone else's experience. Owning another's life means perpetuating their story. If it is one of lack, doubt, and fear, we focus on those aspects until they become our own experience. And so on.

As we transform old patterns and break away from old stories to write new ones, we find that trust is very much alive and well. Of course it is because we know there is always two sides, yes? We can then choose to enhance one or the other. Focussing on trust makes it a strong and very real state in our daily life.

Trust your truth. Trust your intuition.

I'll leave you with a quote from a super model who knows a little something about living an abundant and happy life. Plus, she is super shiny, too.

"The more you trust your intuition, the more empowered you become, the stronger you become, and the happier you become."
Gisele Bündchen

11.2 Living Intuition

You are merging now. You are in a state of complete trust and flow, guided by your intuition. You are aware and listening inward, conscious of your feelings and how you respond to your external world. Every step, every moment, every breath is in alignment with the essence of who you are. Any rift in your resonance is dissolved with clarity. You are sincerely committed to your best vibrations. Nothing and no one can change that. Your awareness is heightened to the degree that you remain connected to your loving heart space always.

Living intuition means that you are in an effortless and ever-allowing state of trusting. You remain aligned with your inner guide.

Know that when change is afoot, deep-seated emotions will surface. Allow it all. Keep riding out emotional upheavals with patience as you come into your new way of being, and continue to drop deeper into trust, as you are guided into unknown territory. Trust that your intuition has your back and the only time things get messy, are those times when you fail to take responsibility, or revert back to blaming etc. You will default until you stop. It is that simple.

Everything is going to change for you when you choose to live intuitively. Living intuition is an entirely new way of perceiving, relating, and behaving in the world, so your old world will fall away thread by thread. Remind yourself often that you are safe to do so.

Living intuition does not mean there will be no challenges, it just means you respond differently to them. Your gratitude for them will grow, and with this practice you will overcome obstacles with greater ease and even grace. You are gradually embodying all aspects inspired by love, and grace is one of the sweetest.

You no longer judge yourself harshly or condemn yourself for having "attracted" something undesirable into your life; rather, you know you are teaching yourself endlessly to become your best self.

There is constant peace in living intuitively. If this underlying peace is lost, you now have the tools you require to bring that peace back. Simple.

When living your intuition, you respect yourself and others, but do not sacrifice your energy for anyone, because you would never expect another to do that for you. You can only be responsible for yourself and in so doing, you guide others into this same sovereign state of being. You are no longer looking to be saved, but are able to ask for help when it is required.

Living intuition means you are in a constant state of forgiveness, no longer attacking or blaming. If you do, you catch it instantly, because you can feel the pain of your actions. You hold others in the light of your love, always, and breathe deeper breaths of compassion.

Be aware of subtle ways in which you can project a fantasy on to another person. As wonderful as it might feel in the moment, you can never control another person's free will, nor should you. This act is one of trying and resisting. You have decided you want a situation to unfold differently and you know what is best for the other person.

Living intuition means you trust you are being guided in the right direction, into the right places and meeting the right people. If you catch any stress or struggle, you can immediately re-arrange your thinking and breathe your way out of it.

Living intuition is subtle and oh so beautiful.

11.3 Oneness

This lesson gets a bit science-y. It is metaphysics meets physics. An unlikely pairing, perhaps, nevertheless, it is happening. Einstein said it best. "The more I learn, the more I realise how much I do not know." So, what was once thought impossible, like flying, becomes possible.

I am not a scientist but find Quantum Mechanics fascinating. It studies motion in sub-atomic particles from a mathematical perspective and is the domain of some of humanity's deepest thinkers. Within a related field called Quantum Coherence is the study of particle entanglement which shows particles communicating with each other instantaneously across huge distances, which could support a "one mind" hypothesis. Could this communication be the basis of evolution?

Evolution certainly has its gaps, but essentially what we know is that once one member of a species adapts for its survival, the entire species jumps up. Is this jump miraculous or quantum coherence? A species does not have a big meeting, sit down and decide another claw is needed to dig bugs out of the trees, they evolve over time. And that same process is happening to us. Every day.

****

Have you ever wondered where your thoughts come from? I have. After my early awakenings, I recall walking down a street in Vancouver, thinking about thought asking, "Where do you come from? How am I hearing you and receiving you?" What followed was an image of a radio tower transmitter and waves being transmitted through my brain. Weird, maybe, but pretty accurate when it comes to understanding how thoughts are shared, but where do they come from? We conceive them.

****

The simplest definition of consciousness is that it means to be awake, aware of "self". According to quantum physics, everything in the knowable universe is wave form and particle, and thought influences these wave and particle forms, in particular when studied in the form of the human body, like epigenetics, which is used to describe anything that influences an organism's development, except DNA. What studies suggest, for example, is that loving thoughts have a positive effect on the body, like increasing serotonin, while worrisome thoughts have a negative effect, i.e., raising blood pressure.

So, let's talk about consciousness again as the awareness that we are, as everything and nothing. As we continue to move along this timeline we have created, we are all becoming more evolved and becoming more aware, or more conscious. What does becoming more conscious involve? It involves becoming more loving and unified.

There has been a lot of reference to density in this guidebook. You have been transforming dense emotions, experienced as fear, judgment, jealousy, anger, and so on, throughout, if you have been doing the exercises. These are lower frequency energetic wavelengths and hopefully, you have decided you do not want to experience them anymore because they are not fun. They make you sick, weary, and miserable. In order to be happy and healthy, you are consciously transforming lower energy forms into higher ones through your intention to do so. That act uplifts you, and the ripple into the collective has begun.

"Human thought forms, as a part of energy in consciousness, are some of the most influential of all energies in our cosmos, much greater than that of the combined energy of all the suns in our universe. This is because thought forms always contain consciousness, and consciousness is part of the original source energy for the existence of all that is.

Learning to harness the power of your thoughts through practices like meditation, contemplation, and prayer, along with increasing high vibrational thoughts associated with unconditional love and compassion will facilitate the Great Change in global consciousness. This Great Change is simply a remembering of this universal truth – we are all One Love.

We all originated from the same source of Love that permeates everything, and beckons us to reunite to create a new energy on earth. This new energy that will make war, famine, poverty, and strife something we only read about in history books, and will make us wonder – Why did we wait so long?"

Keith R. Holden M.D.

Let's stop waiting.

11.4 Nature

We all live together on Earth. Whether you believe you chose to live here or not, does not matter. This planet is your home. There are many opportunities to learn and grow when relating lovingly to your home.

If you live in a city, make sure you find time every day to connect with nature. If possible, take a moment to stand barefoot, on grass, and do a little mini-meditation. Plant your feet firmly on the ground and feel your feet on the soil. Breathe deeply, close your eyes, or at least, lower and soften your gaze. As you breathe deeply, imagine the ground beneath you is a sponge absorbing your body's tension. With every inhale, imagine your body drawing Earth's energy up through the soles of your feet. With every exhale, soften the edges of your body, and let go of any tension. Stick with it until you feel considerably more relaxed, or revitalised.

Make it a "thing". If you work with other people in an office, tell your friends and colleagues about the benefits of daily outdoor time and see if you can get them to join you on your outdoor escapades. Lead them in a mini-meditation if you are guided to do so. Make plans to have lunch outside, weather permitting, and feel free to explain the benefits of spending time in nature.

Like meditation, nature helps to calm the mind, soothe the nervous system and heal the body. Basically, anything that calms and quiets the mind helps heal the body. As we learned in the previous lesson; negative thinking distorts the body's natural functions and creates illness. Stress creates illness. So, share the love in your workplace and play an active role in creating more harmonious environments.

Do not rush your time outdoors. Actively use whatever time to unwind and detach from your daily chores or tasks. Walk for walking's sake, not just to get to a destination. Observe the pace of the world around you, notice the breeze delicately brush your skin, feel the air moving in and out of your lungs, and be mindful of your feet gliding along the sidewalk.

When you learn to slow down enough, everything becomes a meditation. Your inner quietude allows you to enjoy the simplicity and magnitude of being alive. The so-called simple things you used to take for granted become extraordinarily beautiful. Relish your decision to "take time out" from your busy-ness to joyfully give thanks to the planet you are living on.

Light Beam Walking Meditation

You can do this meditation anywhere you are, whether sitting at your meditation station, riding a bicycle, sitting on public transport, or walking. It is a great way to consciously spread love and light into the environment around you, specifically onto dense energy areas like military bases, or hospitals.

While you are walking, soften your gaze and begin to breathe deeply. Relax the edges of your body and lengthen your spine. Establish a comfortable, steady focus and rhythmic walking pattern (if you are walking).

Begin to imagine a massive beam of light coming down from the sun into the crown of your head. See this sparkling golden light fill your body as it continues to beam down on you from above. Once you are filled with light, begin to radiate this light into the earth, like the roots of a tree. Expand the light from your heart all around you, as far out as you can imagine.

Do this meditation whenever you feel like it, but especially if you feel weighed down, or notice yourself judging the world around you. This is the perfect meditation to lighten up.

If you notice any heaviness, or aches or pains in the body arise while being "out in the world", imagine using this same sparkling light beam to dissolve and heal your body. Play around with this form of self-healing. It requires practice and mental focus. You can concentrate the light on specific areas of the body and clear your energy field of anything you might have picked up along the way.

Disclaimer: Always use your intuition when it comes to physical sensation and your body's well-being. Always reach out for help if you are guided to do so and seek professional medical advice if you are unsure about your physical health and safety.

11.5 Freedom

You are free. The system spoken about in Step 1 would have us believe otherwise but we know better now. We made the system so we can change it. Are you starting to see? Are you starting to remember? Even the word re-member means you are putting yourself back together again, through every experience you create, you are ushering in your own awakening and holding space for others to do the same.

Once you wake up from the dream of forgetfulness, piece by piece, moment by moment, you re-member; you connect the

271

dots; you remember why you came here; you remember that it is safe for you to own your darkness because you are light and ultimately, once your eyes are open wide enough and you begin to feel it all from a loving perspective, you remember you are simply here to have fun and create more fun and more after that! You are here to live in bliss with your soul family and to experience unimaginable boundless joy. Whoop-ah!

There are plenty of peeps living it already and, they are waiting for you. They are the ones that smile at you in the street for no reason. They are the ones that show up when you least expect it, and when you need a helping hand. It is you. It is all you, finally starting to show up for yourself because you are remembering how. It is Love. It is all just Love. Love is freedom because it is free and there is an infinite resource of it within us all. We just got blinded temporarily by fear. By the power of our own minds, we tricked ourselves into believing fear was real, and that we were limited, finite and that one day our light might go out. But it is not true. The love that we feel is never truly gone. The light that we are can never go out completely. We may choose to dim it temporarily with distractions and distortions of our own making, just for the fun and challenge of it.

We are like ever blossoming flowers, infinite colours and shades, sizes and shapes, some with prickly thorns for stems and others smooth, delicate; all very beautiful, with a unique fragrance and lifespan.

Never give up. Freedom, like everything else we have discussed, is a feeling within you. A resonant knowing; a flutter in your heart; tears of relief and welcoming joyful exuberance. At long last, you have had enough of the tiresome, senselessness of darkness and the sweet smell of freedom overwhelms your senses. You are finally ready to enjoy this life again. You know Truth, because you know your ever-expanding resonance and this, your own unique vibrational essence and ability to Love All unconditionally will and has, finally set you free.

11.6 Relaxation State

Chillin': The art of doing nothing without getting bored.

The above is a caption I came across on Instagram. I do love social media, mainly because it is a new portal of creation and connectivity, assisting in the global awakening, obviously, by our design.

Relaxation is not laziness, in fact, laziness is another word we could probably redefine or get rid of all together, as we come to see there is nothing wrong with doing nothing. In fact, as a collective, we need to slow right down, it is a needed part of the expansion of consciousness. Again, it is a weird paradox. The more you relax, the more you get done. Now, that is multi-dimensional living, but let's save that for another book, or an entire encyclopaedia.

I have written about the need to relax already, but will do so again. Relaxation is key, indeed, you pretty much want to feel relaxed all the time. If you are not relaxed, you are most likely stressing, which means you are still being triggered by your circumstances and we know this does not feel good. Being tense does not feel nice. This lesson reinforces the need to keep tabs on your state of relaxation until it has become a constant, familiar vibration.

Like right now, I am feeling kind of tired, so instead of trying to rush to finish this book, I am going to take a nap.

****

And now, I am at an airport, about to board a flight back from Singapore. Before that I was in Bali where the majority of this book was written. A series of events called me to Bali, and being one who follows her intuition, I answered the call. The information and energy needed to pen "The Fearless Life Guide" was provided to me there in a place where relaxation is a way of life.

****

Through relaxation, you can connect more readily and strengthen the link between your conscious self, your highest purpose and the physical body. There is no room for stress or worry when you are relaxed.

Corpse Pose, or Savasana, is a yoga posture. It is the final position, and people think I am joking when I say it is the most difficult pose to master, because it means to die. Die to the illusion and rest in peace. That is what the relaxation state asks of you. Stop reacting and being swayed and pulled by the external world and act from within your eternal rested state.

If you are not chillin', if you are not relaxed, you are not fully in the flow. You remain distracted. Obviously some distractions are fun, but plenty are not. It is up to you to discern the difference.

Be diligent with this one. As a collective, our ability to relax is our gateway to remembering how to love again and ultimately heal ourselves. People who report having freed themselves from one disease or another, almost unanimously report the need to rid stress from their lives. You cannot do that if you are not able to relax.

You know it all already, just silence the doubting voices and stop thinking you need someone's approval, or permission, to relax. You have the key and always have had. Go ahead, unlock your door to freedom and let yourself relax. You will surprise yourself when you stop stressing about making plans and trying to figure it all out. You will be amazed at how simple it was all along, and how beautiful it turns out to be when you let go and forgive yourself for ever thinking you did not know. Forgive yourself for ever thinking you could not be free, or that it wasn't safe for you to relax. It turns out to be the safest place for you to be, and in this state of total ease and serenity all your dreams lay waiting to blossom for you. Allow them to. Be peaceful now. Relax.

11.7 Sharing, Caring & Contribution

Now that you are chilled and confident in your ability to relax in pretty much any situation you find yourself in, it is time to share your abundant love vibes with those who are not so chilled out yet. They need your easy going vibrations, probably more than they realise. If they are coming into contact with you, it is because, whether conscious of it or not, they need you. They might not need any wise words, and certainly not advice, but they need your vibrations. You will hold space for them and radiate light. You are going to imagine them as powerful beings, filled with all that star power. You are going to respect them, listen to them, and be present for them. Mainly, you are just going to love the heck out of people until they feel more relaxed.

You are not going to judge, or tell anyone what they have to do to fix themselves. You are not going to pretend you have all the answers, because you do not. They have the answers for themselves. By holding space and radiating your light, you are helping them in the most subtle and powerful way. Whenever you start thinking someone should change, remind yourself that is a judgment. It is not up to anyone to please you. Instead of thinking they need to change, practice seeing them in their happy place, however you can imagine it. Your only job is to love people and practice staying in your happy place. That is pretty much it. The rest is up to them and every being on this planet is more than capable of choosing for themselves.

On another note, you are absolutely here to support the people who need you. Like, the people who are not getting enough food, or indeed, the people your intuition is guiding you to help. Is your intuition saying go to Africa and build some houses, or start a community project to grow veggies, or, get the kids involved in making meals for some people who are hungry? Whatever it is, start answering the call of your intuitive guide. You will feel marvellous and any obstacles you assume might be there, will fall away. Stop making excuses.

Remember the lesson, Overflowing Generosity? This is where you spill that generosity all over the place. Sharing your own uniqueness is the most important lesson within this text. Stop hiding in fear and start sharing. Be easy about it. You do not need to look for opportunities or needs, they will appear when you are relaxed and self-responsible. Everything you desire will appear once you have transformed the energy blocking you, and fulfilling your dreams is your service to the world. Feeling compassion and love for humanity is your service to the world. Dissolving guilt and shame is your contribution; and you are only getting started. Just imagine all of the wonderful things you could do: the hungry mouths fed, the poor uplifted into abundance, and the greedy softened into over-flowingly generous. Imagine it.

You are responsible to this world not because it is the right thing to do, or because it will look good in your portfolio, but because you are the world. The problems you see are yours to fix inside yourself first.

To care is in your favour. To contribute as much as you can is in your favour. You know this. Holding back, buying into the illusion of lack and separation is not helping anyone. Pretending to be a victim is not helping anyone. Rise into your power so you can be the happiest, most radiant version of yourself. That is your highest service to humanity. Do not settle for anything less.

11.8 What To Expect

This is it, my friends. You did it. As far as what to expect goes, well, you tell me? Are you going to go on being the victim, believing life is hard, unfair and unforgiving? Or, are you going to take responsibility, own and master your mind so you can create a life of love and abundance? It is your choice; all the power lies within you. No matter what you choose. Know you are loved.

BONUS LESSON
Relationships

You can gauge the progress of your inner work, not only by how good you feel consistently, but by the harmony and increased awareness you experience in all your encounters. How you relate to yourself is constantly being tested by how you relate to others. Every person you meet, every relationship you have is an assignment.

When your relationships become harmonious, you are making great strides. When you speak up and voice your truth, if only to yourself, you have come a long way. Keep paying attention to the people who trigger you, they are your teachers. Pay attention to the people you aspire to be like, they are your guiding lights. Make everyone in the world your friend and recognise the other is you.

Listen to, and feel your energy in every situation. Tame your thoughts. Keep meditating, stay conscious and keep exploring your inner world; it is All There Is.

Exercises

Step 11. Rest & Relaxation

Exercise A.

Choose one area in your life where you are still experiencing worry and be prepared to discuss.

Exercise B.

Spend some time in meditation, focussing on being filled and surrounded by light. Once in stillness, ask yourself for intuitive guidance. Sit quietly and pay attention to what comes up. When you have finished, write down any insights, words or experiences. Be prepared to share with The Fearless Life Tribe.

Exercise C.

Take a moment to stand on the Earth, ideally barefoot, on grass, and do a little mini-meditation. Plant your feet firmly on the ground and feel your feet on the soil. Breathe deeply, close your eyes, or at least, lower and soften your gaze. As you breathe deeply, imagine the Earth is a sponge absorbing your body's tension. With every inhale, imagine your body drawing the Earth's energy up through the soles of your feet and with every exhale, soften the edges of your body and let go of any tension. Stick with it until you feel considerably more relaxed and calmly revitalised.

Do this every day for a week and note any differences.

Exercise D.

Be as honest as possible. As a daily practice for a whole week, every time you react to an emotional trigger, i.e., get upset with someone or notice your thoughts attacking/blaming/judging someone, as soon as you have noticed the reaction either physically or mentally, pull back and spend one minute either laying down in relaxation or sitting in meditation focussing on deep breathing.

Be prepared to share your experience.

Exercise E.

What kind of service inspires you? How or where do you see yourself adding value to the world? What ideas come up? Write it all down. Be willing to share.

Exercise F.

Give at least one thing away today. It can be as simple as a smile. Be conscious of your giving. Pay attention to how it feels. Be prepared to discuss.

Exercise G.

Creation project. Write a story or make a film about your transformational journey. Where did you start? What challenges did you face and overcome? Where are you now? What kind of life are you creating? Be willing to share this not only with The

Fearless Life Tribe, but publicly, either as a blog or vlog on a social media site.

You did it!

Final Insight

Lighten up. Play. Have fun. Laugh. That is it for the final insight. I think we have gone well and truly deep enough. Now, just go be free.

BONUS LESSON
Pant like a Dog Breathing Exercise

It is in the title. Stick out your tongue and pant like a dog. That is it. To do this, you have to pump your diaphragm rather fast and force the exhale, similar to Breath of Fire. Go on! Laugh at yourself. For the most part, people take themselves way too seriously and do not laugh enough. Laugh more; this breathing exercise will help. It is also energising when you need a pick me up. Do it in front of people; I dare you.

Never Ending Story

Life is a perpetual state of learning, expanding, learning, expanding and on and on it goes. It never ends. Whatever you choose to focus on, however you decide to feel, you will reach your destination. You are there now, and you are already creating a new focus.

Your feel good dreams are waiting for you. All you need to do is believe in your power to really be them. Feel your feelings as you confidently move through life. Be the empowered creator. Be willing to give it all away, in the name of Love. Therein lies your mastery and true potential. Once you really let go of wanting anything at all, you will fall back and be caught by the most miraculous and loving arms; your own. The part of you that always knew you were born to be free.

Go live it.

****

As I write these final words, tears come to my eyes. I am done. And so are you. We made it. And we, together, are going to live in paradise; in the utopia of our own loving imagination; and we're bringing everyone along with us.

I love you unconditionally. I am infinitely thankful to you and so deeply grateful for this epic, eternal life.

Okay now. Deep breath. Wipe my tears. Pant like a dog and laugh it off. I am going to go play now. Namaste.

M. J. Robertson was born in Chatham, Ontario, Canada. After leaving home for the University of British Columbia in Vancouver, she experienced a series of spiritual awakenings. Since that time, M.J. has heeded the call of her intuition to create a new way of living *The Fearless Life* on Earth.

An author and speaker, she is also the founder of All To Love Ltd., www.alltolove.com a company dedicated to her vision of a new paradigm. M.J. hosts her *Diving Deep* Yoga and Surf holidays in exotic tropical locations throughout the year. She is also a yoga and meditation expert at an award winning well-being retreat in the UK.

Having personally surrendered to the transformational power of love, it is with a sincere and compassionate heart that she shares her message with the world through this divinely guided material.

Dedication

This material is dedicated to Love.

Thank you to my family and friends. You have shaped, loved, supported, and encouraged me on my path. I am deeply and over-flowingly grateful.

To the people of this world: May you find it in your hearts to forgive it all and claim your Star Power.

Made in the USA
Columbia, SC
26 December 2017